*Hampton Court*

# PALACE

# Hampton Court
# PALACE

*The* OFFICIAL *Illustrated* HISTORY

LUCY WORSLEY and DAVID SOUDEN

HISTORIC ROYAL PALACES   in association with   **MERRELL**

**LONDON • NEW YORK**

# Hampton Court
# PALACE

*The* OFFICIAL *Illustrated* HISTORY

## CONTENTS

## THE TUDOR PALACE

# THE BAROQUE PALACE

# THE PALACE IN THE MODERN AGE

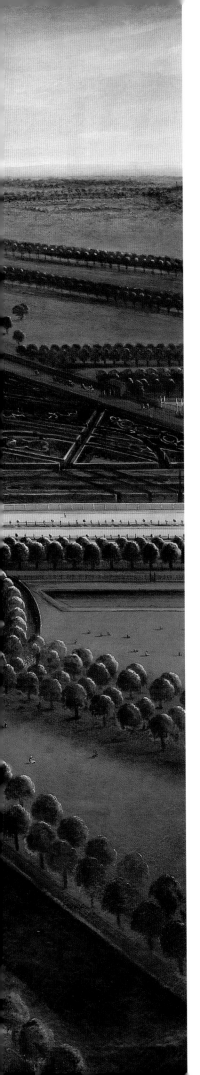

*1. A detail from A view of Hampton Court by Leonard Knyff, which provides a bird's-eye view of the palace and gardens in around 1705. In the centre of the picture is the complex of palace buildings: the further half is the remaining portion of the magnificent red-brick palace built in the reign of Henry VIII, the closer half is the newly built Baroque palace containing the royal apartments. The setting was as magnificent as the buildings, with the avenues in Home Park in the foreground focusing on the elaborate Great Fountain Garden, the formal layout of the King's Privy Garden on the left and the intricate Wilderness on the right. Although some of the garden features have altered, and the surrounding area has been developed, this is still recognizably the view one would see today.*

# Introduction

HAMPTON COURT PALACE is one of the best-known buildings in Britain. Its great West Front is one of the country's most recognizable edifices and the palace is inextricably linked to Henry VIII, one of the most famous if one of the most frightening of English monarchs. Today the palace is ranked among the top historic attractions in the country, as it has been for almost two centuries.

The palace is one of the world's most intriguing buildings. Its 1,300 rooms are spread over 6 acres (2.4 ha) in a gargantuan complex of courtyards, cloisters and chambers. Hampton Court is really two palaces: the sixteenth-century Tudor building constructed for Cardinal Wolsey and Henry VIII, and the late-seventeenth-century Baroque palace commissioned by William III and Mary II. The buildings are set within 60 acres (24 ha) of some of the most magnificent and most frequently visited British gardens. Many parts of these gardens, including the world-famous Maze, are precious survivals from a great age of gardening three centuries ago.

Hampton Court Palace can be read as a textbook of architectural history; it was also the setting for many nationally important events. Here Cardinal Wolsey entertained his king and foreign ambassadors. Henry VIII and most of his six wives held court in its grand apartments. William Shakespeare and his players performed in the Great Hall, and the Authorized Version of the Bible was conceived here. William and Mary brought French court etiquette and a new architectural style to the palace after 1689. In the eighteenth century, Hanoverian fathers and sons argued violently amid its splendours. The court stopped using the palace after 1737 and it became instead a retirement home for courtiers and diplomats "by the grace and favour" of the sovereign. They shared it with an increasing number of tourists. Since 1838, when Queen Victoria opened it to the public, Hampton Court has become a magnet for millions of visitors from Britain and abroad.

There were always quirky and unexpected characters alongside the grand royal residents – whether Sikh princesses who campaigned for women's suffrage or William III's chocolate cook – not to mention the hundreds of people who got lost in the Maze. Today the palace is the busy workplace of building surveyors, curators, conservators, gardeners, accountants and operational staff. Hampton Court is looked after by Historic Royal Palaces, an independent charity charged with conserving the 'unoccupied' royal palaces and educating people about them. We are all guardians of the proud tradition that is described in these pages.

# Life *at* COURT

*2. In this perspective view of the Great Hall engraved by John Vardy in 1749 from a drawing by William Kent, the interior is shown as it might have appeared in the reign of Henry VIII for the reception of foreign ambassadors.*

*3. The arrival of Charles II and his bride Catherine of Braganza at Hampton Court in May 1662. This is one of a series of six prints by Dirk Stoop that illustrated the journey of the new Queen from Lisbon to London. It is a vivid illustration of the scale of the royal court when on the move.*

To understand Hampton Court Palace, one has to understand the court life and the etiquette that underpinned it. The household of the king, the royal court, was for many centuries the political centre of the nation. English kings had many houses, and the court moved with them. Where the monarch resided, there was the court, and people of high social standing expected to participate in it as courtiers. These houses were physical expressions of the logistics required to service a vast number of people and of the ceremonial that was focused on royalty. Until the cost finally proved unsupportable in the 1670s, courtiers expected to receive board and lodging at court in return for their attendance on the king. At court, royal power was exercised. Patronage and favour were given to those who pleased the monarch, or taken away from those who displeased him. All attention was centred on the monarch, who may actually have been seen by few but whose presence was tangible.

## Royal houses

The biggest and best survivor from the period, Hampton Court was only one among many royal palaces in Tudor England. Henry VIII owned over sixty houses and the court would visit them for periods varying from a few hours to a few months (fig. 3). Over time different royal palaces developed different functions: in London the Palace of Westminster was for parliament, Whitehall Palace for government, St James's Palace was the official seat of the monarchy and the Tower of London was used as a refuge in times of danger and as the ceremonial location the night before a coronation. The palace of Hampton Court came to be used primarily for summertime pleasure, relaxation and sport, especially hunting.

This pattern of movement survives to some extent for the Royal Family today. The Queen and her court are at Buckingham Palace for business, at Windsor for weekends, at Balmoral in the summer for holidays and at Sandringham for Christmas.

Between court visits Hampton Court Palace would be closed up and maintained by a skeleton resident staff. Only after the court abandoned it in the eighteenth century did the palace become home to a large number of permanent residents.

## A place at court

Who came to court and what would they have expected? Ambassadors arriving from a foreign monarch, a nobleman hoping to introduce a son or

daughter to good society, or an expert cook or tailor looking for royal patronage had very different experiences at Hampton Court Palace. The building itself was designed to restrict access to the king or queen and to channel people to the spaces appropriate to their rank, keeping them in their proper place both physically and psychologically.

The king on his throne sat at the centre of a vast and slowly revolving array of functionaries: personal attendants, councillors, visiting members of the aristocracy and their servants, sightseers and tradesmen. The long chains of rooms or *enfilades* in the palace, one leading into another, acted like a filter. The guards at each successive doorway prevented the unworthy from penetrating into the king's inner rooms. Clothes played a vital part in the guards' decision whether to let someone pass, and clothing consumed a high proportion of a courtier's income. In Tudor times a black suit appropriate for court was worth a year's rent on a London house.

The first obstacle to pass through was the gatehouse, where entry was strictly controlled by the

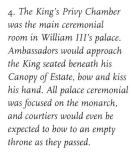

*4. The King's Privy Chamber was the main ceremonial room in William III's palace. Ambassadors would approach the King seated beneath his Canopy of Estate, bow and kiss his hand. All palace ceremonial was focused on the monarch, and courtiers would even be expected to bow to an empty throne as they passed.*

porters. A seventeenth-century rule book produced for the household of the future Charles II contains their job description: "there shall be continually one or more of them diligently attending the Gate, and shall suffer none to enter in, but such as be enrolled in a List". Later in the same century, William III lived in fear of his many enemies and constructed the Barrack Block, outside the Great Gatehouse, to accommodate his Household Guard.

Once inside the gates, the visitor found two main departments of the court: the Lord Chamberlain's department, which was responsible for the running of the state rooms, and the Lord Steward's department (fig. 5), responsible for the 'below stairs' areas of the palace such as the kitchens. When the king was in residence, milling crowds pushed through the courtyards. There could be as many as 800 members in attendance at Henry VIII's court. Provisioning the royal household placed such a huge burden on the surrounding countryside that the court could not remain for long. During the reign of Mary I, there were dire consequences when the court became

trapped at Hampton Court because the Queen was suffering a phantom pregnancy and could not travel. The palace moat became an open cesspit.

The centre of life for most of the lower-ranking members of the court was the Great Hall, where in Tudor times they dined in two shifts in the middle of the day. Senior courtiers ate in the adjoining Great Watching Chamber (fig. 6). Henry VIII himself ate in stately isolation in his dining room with courtiers looking on (fig. 7); his dishes were produced in his own Privy Kitchen rather than in the Great Kitchens serving the Great Hall. In the later seventeenth century, the cost of feeding the whole of the royal household became prohibitive and the privilege was abolished for all but the grandest. Courtiers then had to make their own arrangements.

## Royal apartments

A visitor of high rank in Tudor times would expect to pass through the Great Hall into the more exclusive rooms beyond; similarly, a visitor in later centuries would climb the King's or Queen's Staircases to

ABOVE 7. *Henry VIII dining in his Presence Chamber. The King would sit alone at his table on a dais, surrounded by his court and served on bended knee. The figures on the left holding staves are his senior court officers, the members of the King's Chamber.*

OPPOSITE 8. *The King's Great Bedchamber was the grandest state room; a room for the Gentlemen of the Bedchamber was next door. In 1699 William III announced that in future all ambassadors were to be received at Hampton Court rather than at his London palaces, and he probably received ambassadors in the bedchamber, just as Charles II had done.*

reach the State Apartments above. These were the rooms where the king's or queen's occasional presence could be expected at set times for the reception of ambassadors or guests, or as the monarch passed through the palace to visit the Chapel.

To enter these rooms, the most important in the palace, visitors had to negotiate the Guard Chamber and the formidable Yeomen of the Guard (fig. 9). In the sixteenth century, the guards in the Great Watching Chamber prevented unauthorized access to Henry VIII's private rooms. In the seventeenth century, William III's guards slept in the Guard Chamber of the King's State Apartments. In the eighteenth century, Sir John Vanbrugh even incorporated the figures of the guards themselves into his design for the fireplace in the Queen's Guard Chamber (fig. 114). Their job was to ensure that no "idle, mean or unknown persons" entered the state rooms beyond.

The room behind the Guard Chamber was known at different times as the Audience Chamber, Privy Chamber or Presence Chamber. This was the room in which the king or queen sat beneath a Canopy of Estate and where ambassadors might have been presented, bowing to the monarch and kissing his or her hand. The next room in the sequence was the Eating Room, in which the monarch might dine in public in front of a select group of courtiers. The Eating Room was followed by a further Privy Chamber or Audience Chamber. This was the most important ceremonial room in the palace, where the king or queen conducted most of the royal audiences or receptions (fig. 4). The monarch would 'withdraw' from the presence of all but the highest-ranking members of the royal household into the next room, the Withdrawing Room. Here, select visitors were given privileged access: they were allowed to see the

The Armoury, Hampton Court Palace.

monarch in a less formal setting, perhaps to play cards or for conversation. In the eighteenth century, the 'drawing room' became both a place and an event, the latter an entertainment with cards and tea drinking where the king or queen would circulate for an hour or so to meet courtiers and visitors.

The honour of being present in the drawing room was sometimes dearly bought. Courtiers were constrained by the rules of ceremony at all times. Among eighteenth-century commentators, Alexander Pope described with barbed wit how "the life of a Maid of Honour [one of the personal attendants of the queen] was of all things the most miserable ... they must simper an hour and catch cold in the Princess's apartment, from thence to dinner, with what appetite they may", while Lord Hervey spoke wearily of the tedium of life at court, where the same predictable events took place at the same time each day.

## Bedchamber politics

Beyond the Withdrawing Room lay the Bedchamber (fig. 8). Henry VIII constructed a new bedchamber at Hampton Court Palace to complete the sequence of his rooms: Great Watching Chamber, Presence Chamber, Dining Chamber and Withdrawing Chamber. A specially built tower contained the room for his bed, his adjacent bathroom, his study and library. Henry's personal attendants surrounded him constantly, providing the most intimate services. In 1528 Thomas Heneage apologized to Cardinal Wolsey that he had been unable to come to a meeting because "there is none here but Master Norris and I to give attendance upon the King's Highness when he goeth to make water in his bedchamber". The rule books ordered the King's body servants to do their duties in a "humble, reverent, secret and lowly manner ... not pressing his Grace nor advancing themselves" further than the King required. Yet Henry found that too many courtiers, suitors and officials nevertheless achieved access to his most private rooms. At Hampton Court he added a whole new suite – his 'Secret Lodgings' – in order to get away from them. This suite overlooked his Privy Garden to the south, a vital part of the palace in all periods for royal relaxation outdoors.

With the passage of time the court became more formal both in terms of the variety of spaces it required and its personnel. Henry VIII's personal servants had been among the most powerful men in the land, as they controlled access to him and could speak to him in the most private moments. The Groom of the Stool was the most important courtier of all and attended the king in the close-stool room. William III's close stool (a chamber pot hidden under a padded seat) remains at Hampton Court Palace today (fig. 11). With access to the bedchamber, closet and close-stool room, the Groom of the Stool was inevitably the person closest to the monarch and consequently wielded enormous power, symbolically keeping the key to the bedchamber on a ribbon round his neck. From the seventeenth century, the Bedchamber became a separate department of the court, staffed by Gentlemen and Grooms of the Bedchamber under the Groom of the Stool (later written as Stole). William III's Groom of the Stool was his favourite, Hans Willem Bentinck, Earl of Portland (fig. 10).

By William III's time, the Great Bedchamber was no longer actually used for sleeping. The state bed had become as much a symbol of power as was a throne. The later Stuart monarchs were heavily influenced by the ceremonies at the court of Louis XIV, the Sun King, in France, which included a ceremony of dressing and undressing each morning and evening 'performed' before members of the court and distinguished visitors. William III held a similar *levée* (literally, getting up) in his Great Bedchamber, but he actually slept either in the Little Bedchamber next door or in a room in his cosier private apartments downstairs.

A glimpse of the court's intricate ritual comes from the life of Queen Caroline, wife of George II. When she washed her hands, the Page of the Backstairs brought the basin and ewer but the Bedchamber-Woman set it before the Queen:

> The Bedchamber-Woman pulled on the Queen's gloves, when she could not do it herself. The Page of the Backstairs was called in to put on the Queen's shoes. When the Queen dined in public, the Page reached the glass to the Bedchamber-Woman, and she to the Lady-in-waiting. The Bedchamber-Woman brought the chocolate, and gave it without kneeling.

Despite the formality it was still possible to receive informal or secret visitors. On occasions when discretion was vital, visitors were brought in by the back stairs leading to the king's or queen's private chambers. This circumvented the whole sequence of state apartments and officers guarding their doors. Genuine 'backstairs intrigues' took place on the smaller staircases leading down from William III's State Apartments or leading up to the private rooms of Queen Caroline.

### Courtiers' lodgings

In addition to the royal apartments, the palace always contained accommodation for courtiers. The house

built for Cardinal Wolsey included Base Court, thirty suites of lodgings used for grand visitors (fig. 22); William III's courtiers squabbled over the allocation of lodgings in the newly rebuilt palace at the end of the seventeenth century. These suites of rooms, constantly being altered, enlarged or contracted, eventually became separate apartments used by the residents of the palace who were given permission to live there once the court no longer visited the palace. It is still possible to stay in the palace today in the apartments (one in the Georgian House, one in the Tudor confectioners' office in Fish Court) managed as holiday houses by the Landmark Trust.

From the sixteenth to the eighteenth centuries, life at Hampton Court was sleepy and rural between regular frenetic bouts of court residence, with attendant courtiers, and rebuilding. In the course of 200 years the porters, Yeomen of the Guard, courtiers, Grooms of the Stool and kings themselves performed a complicated dance of ceremony. Life at court changed slowly over the centuries, becoming increasingly elaborate and formal but always remaining magnificent.

# *Before* the PALACE

The Saxon estate of Hampton passes through the hands of the Norman de St Valery family and the Knights Hospitallers before being acquired by Giles, Lord Daubeney in 1494. He builds the house visited by Henry VII and Elizabeth of York.

*12. Aerial view of Hampton Court from the south-east. In ancient times the confluence of the Thames with the lesser rivers of the Mole and the Ember made water transport easy. The plain was free-draining and fertile, if subject to occasional floods.*

*13. The record for the manor of Hampton in the Domesday Book notes that the property had formerly been in the possession of Aelfgar, a Saxon earl. The manor consisted of 1,700 hectares (4,200 acres) and was valued at £39.*

## Origins

Royal connections and evidence of great wealth at Hampton Court long pre-date the Tudor palace. In the reign of Henry VIII, treasure – "Roman money of silver", "plates of silver" and "chains of silver" – was discovered in the flat river plain around Hampton Court and the nearby town of Kingston. This showed that the best-known home of the Tudor king stands on a site that had been the scene of human activity for centuries. The bend of the River Thames as it snakes through the gravel terraces below the Surrey hills provided a perfect location for an ancient settlement (fig. 12). The name 'Hampton' is Saxon in origin, meaning a settlement (*ton*) at the bend of the river (*hamm*). This area was important in Saxon times: King Athelstan was consecrated at Kingston, the town's name itself denoting its significance as the centre of a royal estate.

The Domesday Book, the land survey made for William the Conqueror in 1086, records that Sir Walter de St Valery, a prominent Norman, owned Hampton (fig. 13). His land had declined in value since the Conquest, possibly because it had been exploited and stripped bare by the slow passage of the Norman armies. By introducing sheep, St Valery was gradually able to build up a prosperous estate. Yet generations of St Valerys were lured to distant lands by the medieval passion for crusading to liberate the Christian sites in the Holy Land. It was in Jerusalem that an important change of direction in

Hampton Court's future was determined. Sir Walter de St Valery took part in the first of the series of great crusades in 1096. In 1147–49 his grandson, Reginald, was among the members of the Second Crusade, which succeeded in taking Jerusalem from the forces of Islam. Reginald de St Valery was made a Baron of Jerusalem, a city where succour and hospitality were offered to the visiting knights by a fighting order of monks, the Knights Hospitallers.

The Knights Hospitallers' original purpose was to nurse wounded crusaders, but in the late twelfth century they were given permission to help defend the crusaders' castle strongholds. Across Europe, regional priories raised money to be sent to the order's Grand Master (who from 1309 was based in Rhodes after Jerusalem had fallen). By the 1180s, Reginald allowed the Knights Hospitallers, whom he had encountered in Jerusalem, to rent Hampton

This bell, cast in 1479, hangs above Anne Boleyn's Gateway. Its inscription, "Mary, most holy Star of the Sea, come to our aid", suggests that it was originally made for a ship.

In 1485 Giles Daubeney became master of Henry VII's hart (or deer) hounds. Hampton Court was to be a royal hunting park until the start of the nineteenth century.

In 1503 Henry VII's pregnant wife, Elizabeth of York, visited Hampton Court, and died soon after. Her second son, Henry, would become king six years later and in due course would take the property for himself.

14. *The Hospitallers of the Order of St John of Jerusalem, established to care for the sick in the crusades to the Holy Land, owned the manor of Hampton Court for three centuries. Engraving by Philippe Thomassin (1562–1622).*

days a year. It was the centre of a large and important agricultural estate containing 800 acres (324 ha) of arable land and 2000 sheep. There was a permanent warden, assisted by a chamberlain, a baker, a gate-keeper and a chaplain. While the building was a farming centre, it also served an important function as a guest house for grand visitors to the royal court when it was at Byfleet nearby.

After many years, the Knights Hospitallers found it more profitable to give their lease to a sequence of secular owners. The first recorded lease was to John Wode, a favoured royal servant of Edward IV and Richard III. The Knights Hospitallers then returned for ten years, before leasing Hampton Court to the courtier Giles Daubeney in 1494.

## Lord Daubeney's Hampton Court

Giles, later Lord, Daubeney, was one of Henry VII's staunchest supporters, and had spent a period of exile in France before his rise in the wake of Henry VII's accession. He fought bravely at the Battle of Bosworth in 1485, the last episode in the fifteenth-century dynastic Wars of the Roses, which were concluded by the death of Richard III in the battle and the marriage of the Yorkist princess Elizabeth to the victorious Henry Tudor. In 1495 Daubeney became Lord Chamberlain of Henry VII's household, having acquired the manor of Hampton Court as a country house the previous year. The guests he hoped to receive there were the sources of his power and privilege: the royal family.

Daubeney tried but failed to acquire the outright freehold to the manor, but he did win a ninety-nine-year lease from the Knights Hospitallers. He also had the right to "take, alter, transpose, break, change, make and new build" the house according to his wishes. Daubeney took advantage of this to make great improvements to the manor, and some of his work still survives. His workmen completed a court-yard of dwellings (fig. 15), with a gatehouse to the west and a semi-detached kitchen to the north. This is the Great Kitchen that remains today, with an enormous fireplace for spit-roasts in its southern wall (fig. 18). Between the Great Kitchen and Great Hall, which stood side by side, was a serving place from which the waiters took the dishes of food prepared in the one to be consumed in the other. A list made in 1495 records that this Great Hall contained two fixed tables, two long trestle tables, four benches, a cupboard and a railing round the central hearth. Daubeney added a tower to the former chamber block, and according to the inventory the "tower chamber" contained a press for clothes and a "great coffer". This was a truly grand house (fig. 16), fit for entertaining the king and queen.

15. *View down into Clock Court, looking south from the roof of the Great Hall. The bricks set into the surface of the courtyard mark out the position of Daubeney's range, which once stood here. This area was excavated in the 1960s and 1970s.*

Court (fig. 14). The name of one of the new residents is known: Joan, unusually a female member of the order, who later left Hampton to go to a new Hospi-taller community at Buckland in Somerset.

What kind of building did the Knights Hospitallers take over from the St Valerys? It is described in a document of 1338, the 'extent' or measurement of their holding. The house itself stood in an enclosure surrounded by a rectangular moat. There was proba-bly a chamber block and a great hall, traces of which have been found beneath the existing Great Hall. A separate chapel stood to the east. There was also a garden and a pigeon house (vital for providing fresh meat throughout the winter). The prior of the order in England would visit Hampton Court for three

In his negotiations with the Knights Hospitallers, Daubeney managed to extricate himself from the

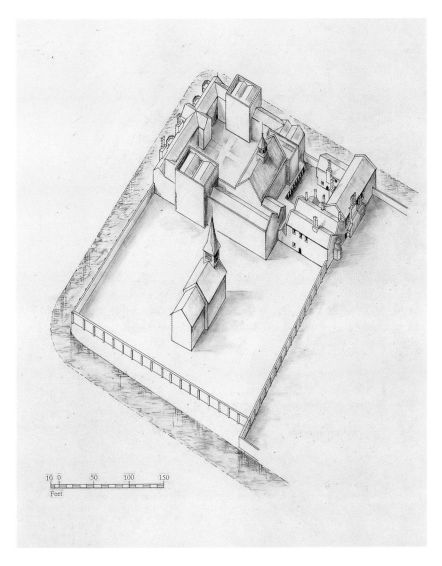

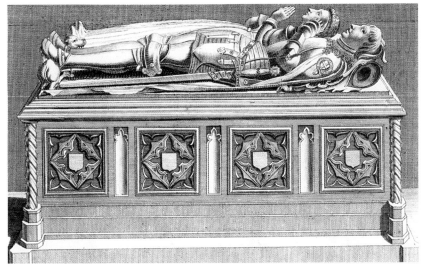

requirement to provide a priest to "sing and minister divine service" in the chapel on their behalf. Today an ancient bell hangs in the tower above the inner gatehouse. Mentioned in a later lease of Hampton Court, it may well have come from the chapel of Daubeney's time or even before.

## Royal visitors

In 1503, Hampton Court was the setting for one of the final scenes in the life of Henry VII's queen, Elizabeth of York. The reserved and financially astute Henry occasionally used Hampton Court as a 'cell', or a retreat for periods of contemplation. On 7 January 1503 the Queen was rowed up the river from Richmond to the manor of Hampton Court in a "great boat" for such a restful visit. Her servants kept the boat moored at Hampton Court for the week of her stay, which passed uncomfortably. Now in her mid-thirties, she was suffering from a difficult pregnancy, while only nine months previously she had learned that her eldest son, Arthur, Prince of Wales, had died in Ludlow.

After leaving Hampton Court, the Queen was taken to the Palace of Westminster where she and the King were to celebrate Candlemas together. On 2 February she gave birth prematurely to a daughter, Catherine, who lived for only a few days. On 11 February the Queen herself died. Henry was bereft, but continued to visit Hampton Court until Daubeney's death in 1508 (fig. 17).

Henry himself died the following year. Hampton Court was soon to be transformed by its next two owners: the great Cardinal Wolsey and Henry VIII, Henry VII's surviving son. Under them it became the palace that is still familiar today.

CARDINAL WOOLSEY

# *Cardinal* WOLSEY'S
# *Hampton* COURT 1514–29

Cardinal Wolsey, Henry VIII's chief minister, acquires Hampton Court and begins to rebuild it as a magnificent palace. His work is intended to impress the great men of Europe, and much of what he built remains to be seen today.

*19. Thomas Wolsey (1472/3–1530), by an unknown artist, late sixteenth century, from an original of c. 1520. Wolsey appears to be overweight in this portrait, and suffered at various times from throat infections, colic, fevers, jaundice and gallstones. He occasionally fell into faints that may have been diabetic comas, and after his arrest he suffered from vomiting and bowel trouble, which also match symptoms of diabetes.*

*20. After Wolsey's fall from grace, his arms in Clock Court with their cardinal's hat and supporting cherubs were covered up and replaced by the arms of Henry VIII. They were rediscovered only in the nineteenth century.*

## Cardinal Wolsey

A terracotta panel set above Anne Boleyn's Gateway in Clock Court shows two cherubs holding up a coat of arms (fig. 20). Above them floats a wide-brimmed hat with many tassels. The arms and the hat – the special headgear of a cardinal of the Catholic Church – belonged to one of Hampton Court's most flamboyant owners, Thomas Wolsey.

Cardinal Wolsey was the last of his type. Great churchmen had been political leaders and prolific builders throughout medieval times until Henry VIII took away much of their power by splitting the Church of England from the international Catholic Church, refusing to recognize the authority of the

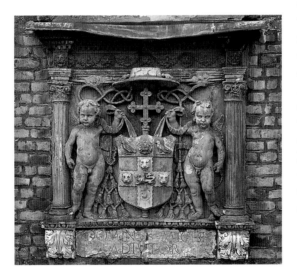

Pope in Rome. Churchmen such as Wolsey, who played a significant role in government, would not be seen in England again. Yet he also had much in common with the princes of his own Renaissance times. He was interested in new artistic and cultural ideas, in the rediscovery of designs and ideas from Classical times, and in effective administration.

Thomas Wolsey (fig. 19) was born in Ipswich, some time late in 1472 or early in 1473. His father was a butcher and grazier and was rich enough to send his son to the school of Magdalen College, Oxford. Through the patronage of the Marquis of Dorset, Wolsey was appointed rector of Limington in Somerset. This was the first rung on the ladder to high office that he was to climb so successfully. The Church was one of the few careers open to clever young men from non-aristocratic backgrounds. It was to some extent a meritocracy, though the patronage of influential friends was important. One of Wolsey's supporters was the Archbishop of Canterbury, whose chaplain he became. By 1507 Wolsey had made the vital transfer to the king's household, becoming chaplain to Henry VII himself. As well as saying Mass, he had administrative tasks to perform and was sent on confidential missions abroad. He found himself equally highly valued by Henry VIII, and received a clutch of bishoprics. By 1515 he was a cardinal, and in 1518 he became the Pope's legate in England.

Wolsey's enduring image is as a brooding and powerful figure, a sinister string-puller on behalf of

The enormous Cardinal spider (Tegenaria guyonii or domestica) is unique to Hampton Court Palace and its environs. It is said to be destined forever to haunt the scene of Wolsey's former greatness.

In his 1742 guidebook to the palace, George Bickham queried why Wolsey included the Emperor Vitellius among the Maiano roundels. He "had not one good quality to recommend him, but like the Cardinal was notorious for his dissolute and luxurious course of life".

Fragments of terracotta decoration from Wolsey's long gallery – shafts and bases of classical columns – were found during the excavation of the Privy Garden in 1993–94.

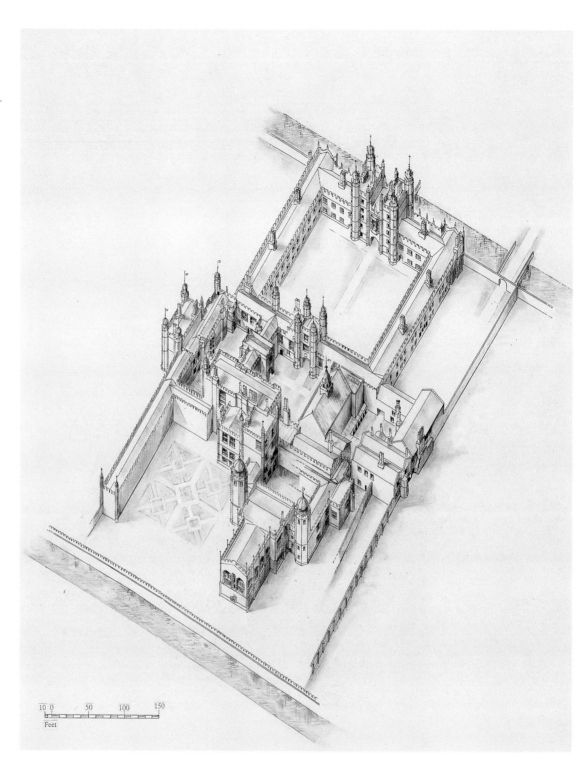

21. *Reconstruction of Wolsey's palace in 1528–29, by Daphne Ford. The parts of the building known only from archaeological investigations have been shown here without doors and windows. Those parts shown with fenestration still survive today.*

10 0    50    100    150
Feet

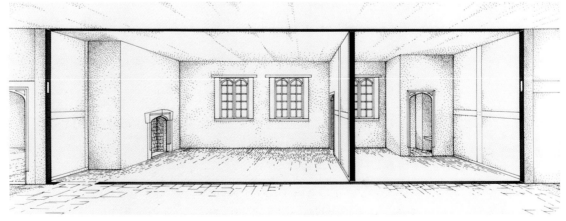

22. *Reconstruction of a double lodging in Wolsey's Base Court, by Daphne Ford. A visitor arriving at Hampton Court entered his rooms from a covered walkway or gallery. He may have found his lodging decorated with tapestries from the Cardinal's collection, or he may even have brought his own hangings with him.*

the Pope. In reality, we know relatively little about his appearance and character. His best-known biographer, George Cavendish, wrote after Wolsey's death in a self-confessed effort to set the record straight about the evil rumours that had grown up around his master. Wolsey's reputation has always been controversial. His talent for statecraft and his industry were prodigious. Cavendish was impressed by the Cardinal's powers of concentration: during negotiations with the French in 1527, Wolsey worked from four o'clock in the morning until four o'clock in the afternoon, yet "never rose once to piss, nor yet to any meat, but continually wrote his letters with his own hands, having all that time his nightcap and kerchief on his head". In addition to his administrative skills, the Cardinal did, however, find the time to have two illegitimate children, a boy and a girl, by his lover Mistress Lark, and publicly acknowledged the boy as his 'nephew'.

Even Wolsey's enemy William Tyndale gave him credit for being "a gay finder out of new pastimes". A prince of the church needed to be able to entertain the great men of Europe. Once Wolsey had become a cardinal, it was even possible that he could aspire to be the second English pope. Indeed, the Venetian ambassador described how Wolsey was "in very great repute – seven times more so than if he were pope". Thomas More, Wolsey's successor as chancellor, described how Wolsey was glorious "very far above

all measure, and that was great pity; for it did harm and made him abuse many great gifts that God had given him". To those writing afterwards, it seemed that Wolsey's great pride and success led inevitably to his terrible fall from power.

Wolsey owned several houses by virtue of his official positions. For example, as Archbishop of York he was entitled to York Place, his house in Westminster – later transformed by Henry VIII into Whitehall Palace. Hampton Court was the first house Wolsey acquired privately, and he did so because he needed an appropriately splendid country house for entertaining. He had probably met Giles Daubeney,

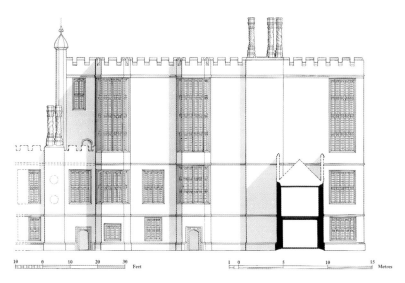

TOP 25. *One of Giovanni da Maiano's eight roundels incorporating the heads of Roman emperors, executed in glazed terracotta. This is the head of the Emperor Augustus.*

ABOVE 26. *These lodgings were created by Wolsey to the east of Clock Court for the royal family after 1522. In 1531 a visitor from Belgrade reported that "there is space for the King to inhabit the centre floor, the Queen the one above and the Princess [Mary] the ground floor". Drawing by Daphne Ford.*

Hampton Court's previous owner, at court. After Daubeney's death, his son was glad to pass Hampton Court on to Wolsey in 1514 in order to clear his father's debts. Wolsey never managed to obtain the freehold as well as the leasehold from the Knights Hospitallers; it fell to Henry VIII, the palace's next owner, to achieve this in due course.

### Wolsey's first phase of work, 1514–22
Wolsey quickly set repairs and improvements in hand under the supervision of Lawrence Stubbs. Stubbs was a priest as well as the skilful administrator of Wolsey's building projects up and down the

country: the colleges he was building at Oxford and Ipswich, another country house at The More in Hertfordshire, and improvements to both Hampton Court and York Place. Wolsey's first phase of work at Hampton Court, built to the west of Daubeney's house, consisted of a whole new courtyard of accommodation, Base Court (fig. 23). Here, thirty pairs of rooms could be dressed with furniture and tapestries (fig. 22) and allocated to guests from all over Europe. Their plan was innovative. Previously lodgings like this had garderobes in towers that protruded from their back walls; at Hampton Court the garderobes and chimneys were built into the thickness of the walls between suites so that the building had a much neater appearance.

The entrance to Base Court was through the imposing Great Gatehouse, still the most instantly recognizable part of the whole palace. However, Wolsey would never have seen it in its current form, as both Henry VIII and Elizabeth I altered it and in the eighteenth century its top two storeys were removed (fig. 24). Before the gatehouse lay one of the most striking features of Wolsey's Hampton Court: its large rectangular moat ditch, excavated for display rather than defence. Lost in subsequent years, the moat was re-excavated early in the twentieth century.

Wolsey added a brand-new, magnificent long gallery extending from the private chambers of Daubeney's house into the garden towards the south-east, the site of the Cartoon Gallery today. The gallery, 60 m (200 ft) long, was used for exercise and conversation and for viewing the gardens. It was especially innovative because of its terracotta ornaments in the new Renaissance style, which incorporated copies of the ancient Roman orders of architecture along with laurel wreaths. Another wonderfully foreign and novel feature of Wolsey's palace was the series of heads of the Roman emperors, made in brightly glazed terracotta (fig. 25). Their Italian sculptor, Giovanni da Maiano, made eight busts for Hampton Court. (Rather confusingly, there are ten set into the palace walls today; the extra pair, Nero and Tiberius, were probably brought from the famous but long-demolished Holbein Gate at Whitehall Palace.) Although well known in Italy, this was a new style of decoration in England but one that was wholly appropriate for a cardinal whose peers were the leading churchmen and princes of Renaissance Europe.

### Wolsey's second phase of work, 1522–28
Wolsey's second phase of building took place in the course of the six years from 1522 (fig. 21). Although no accounts survive for the work, we know that he improved the best chambers of the old house by creating three suites fit for royal occupation. The whole of the east side of Clock Court became a block of

ABOVE LEFT 27. *Fragments of the leather mâché frieze from Wolsey's new rooms of 1526. The design incorporated Renaissance cherubs and a classical vase.*

ABOVE RIGHT 28. *Detail of the ribbed ceiling in Wolsey's rooms in the South Front of the palace, incorporating the Cardinal's badges. This is one of the most precious survivals of interior decoration from the Cardinal's palace. (The present ceiling includes new sections made of fibreglass in 1961 and moulded from the original.)*

RIGHT 29. *A reconstruction of the east end of Wolsey's chapel, by Daphne Ford. Remains of the great double window survive behind Queen Anne's eighteenth-century reredos, which dominates the view today. The stained-glass windows, designed by Erhard Schön from Nuremberg, included the figures of a king and queen praying.*

splendid royal lodgings, intended for Henry's daughter the Princess Mary on the ground floor, Henry VIII himself on the first floor and his first wife Catherine of Aragon on the second (fig. 26). In fact the three of them could not have stayed at Hampton Court simultaneously, as the Princess had a household of 160 and the Queen of 200. Even Hampton Court could not hold all these people in addition to the King's own enormous winter household. The top-floor apartments were the most spectacular, for their windows were enormously high and wide, and would have caught and amazed the eyes of visitors passing through the gatehouse into Clock Court.

In 1526 Wolsey constructed a smaller but still luxurious suite for himself off a little courtyard to the south of Clock Court (fig. 28). His richly panelled rooms contained a decorative frieze made of leather mâché (fig. 27), a mixture of leather and glue that could be moulded to form cherubs, vases and swirls. From his rooms, Wolsey looked out over sunny gardens to the south of the palace. He had fishponds constructed to provide fish for his table; in 1528 Anne Boleyn was to beg him to send her freshwater shrimps and carp from Hampton Court.

Another feature of Wolsey's house, distinguishing it from the houses of other courtiers, was the Chapel and the grand processional route to it. In a king's or cardinal's household, the stately procession from his own chambers to chapel to hear Mass on feast-days was an important ritual. Passing along the gallery, accompanied by his officers, the king or grandee could see and be seen by the throngs of

31. *In this area of 'fictive' or false diaper-work decoration on the external east wall of the Chapel, the black pattern has simply been painted on to the bricks.*

differences are useful to archaeologists today, who can identify the characteristics of a particular period. Although written accounts do not survive for the later phase of Wolsey's building works, it is possible nevertheless to work out that the royal lodgings, his own lodgings and the Chapel were built in one campaign because they share similar bricks. The soft red brick of Wolsey's building was enhanced by patterns in 'diaper-work', diamond-shaped designs picked out in black or over-burnt bricks (fig. 30). This subtle decoration once covered most of the palace, although later repairs have erased or spoiled much of it. However, on the external east wall of the Chapel, one patch of what appears to be diaper-work survives in good condition because it has been sheltered from the elements by later buildings constructed against it. Here the builders tried to deceive the eye by continuing the diaper pattern in black paint rather than by using actual blackened bricks (fig. 31).

One of the most sumptuous occasions at Wolsey's palace was the visit of the French ambassadors in 1527. Cavendish described the visit in great detail in order to record his former master's wealth and hospitality. In their sleeping chambers the French guests found silver vessels from which to drink and eat. Even their candles were extraordinary for the time, both white and yellow in three different sizes. Cavendish described the silver sconces lighting the dining room, probably what is now the Great Watching Chamber behind the Great Hall, the cupboard (literally a board for standing cups upon) holding gold and silver plates, the "tall yeomen" standing by and, above all, Wolsey's spectacular tapestries.

## Wolsey's tapestries

Tapestry in Tudor times was not merely a wall covering, it was a statement of conspicuous consumption (fig. 32). A large, rich tapestry woven with gold and silver thread might cost as much as a battleship. It provided a subtle means of communication between the palace's owner and his guests, as the stories depicted could be unravelled by those with an education in the classics. One of Wolsey's most magnificent purchases was made in the early 1520s when he sent the London merchant Richard Gresham to The Netherlands with 1000 marks to spend on tapestries for eighteen completed rooms at Hampton Court. Wolsey's own closet was hung with cloth of gold, and he ended up with more than 600 tapestries in his collection. An ambassador from Venice described how, when visiting Wolsey, "one has to traverse eight rooms before one reaches his audience chamber, and they are all hung with tapestry, which is changed every week".

This kind of extravagance was expected from a great cardinal, but there were always people ready to criticize a churchman who spent so much on

courtiers and visitors. At Hampton Court, Wolsey constructed a magnificent double-height chapel, with an enormous double window at its east end filled with stained glass (fig. 29). The gallery forming the royal route to the Chapel still survives and is known today as the Haunted Gallery (fig. 51). Beneath it ran a cloister for servants, giving access from courtyard to courtyard. Wolsey's chapel choir was excellent, so fine that in 1519 Henry VIII insisted that some of its members transfer to the King's own singers; the choristers who still practise in the Chapel today are their successors.

Wolsey's Hampton Court was notable for the high quality of both materials and construction. Tudor bricks were by no means uniform in appearance, and their colour and shape varied from batch to batch according to the clay used and the brickmaker. These

material possessions. One of these was John Skelton, who wrote a biting satire about Wolsey. Skelton was both amazed and appalled by Wolsey's tapestries with their fabulous characters and creatures:

> How the world stares
> How they ride in goodly chairs
> Conveyed by elephants
> With laryat garlands
> And by unicorns
> With their seemly horns
> Upon these beasts riding
> Naked boys striding
> With wanton wenches winking!

Churches and cathedrals were falling down, Skelton complained, while Wolsey spent his wealth on tapestry. Skelton even ventured on to the dangerous ground of comparing Wolsey's court to the King's:

> Why come you not to Court?
> To which court?
> To the king's court?
> Or to Hampton Court?
> Nay, to the king's court!
> The king's court
> Should have the excellence
> But Hampton Court
> Hath the pre-eminence!

## Wolsey's fall

There is a satisfying dramatic logic to the theory that the seeds of Wolsey's downfall lay within his greatest successes. Many historians tell the tale of how the proud cardinal made his house unduly and dangerously magnificent, thereby offending the King, who could not bear to be eclipsed. This is the psychological background, we are told, to Henry VIII's finally confiscating Hampton Court from Wolsey in 1528.

However, this is more than misleading. Wolsey's great house was a compliment, not a threat, to the King and Henry had always treated it as if it were his own. Wolsey himself explained: "I should have all this royalty, because I represent the king's majesty's person in all the high courts of this realm, to the terror and keeping down of all rebellious treasons, traitors, all the wicked and corrupt members of this commonwealth." He intended the best rooms at Hampton Court for the King's use. His biographer tells us that it often pleased the King "for his recreation, to repair unto the Cardinal's house, as he did diverse times in the year ... such pleasures were then devised for the king's comfort and consolation as might be invented, or by man's wit imagined".

In the late 1520s, Wolsey appeared to have a golden touch. What brought him down was not Henry's envy but the political scandal that became known as the King's 'great matter'. Like his royal master, Wolsey was to suffer from the King's problems with his first wife.

32. *'The Triumph of Fame over Death', from a set of tapestries depicting the* Triumphs of Petrarch, *woven in Flanders in the early sixteenth century. The figure on the chariot pulled by bulls to the left is Fate or Death, being toppled by the angel with the trumpet. To the right, Fame stands on her chariot drawn by elephants. The ranks of stately figures accompanying the carts include all the heroes of antiquity. This tapestry formed part of Cardinal Wolsey's collection; after Wolsey's death in 1530, Henry VIII took possession of it. This was, and still is, hung in the Great Watching Chamber.*

# *Henry* VIII's
# *Hampton* COURT Palace 1529–47

Henry VIII takes Hampton Court as his own royal palace. Wolsey falls from power. The King turns the building into a vast pleasure palace. Important episodes in the lives of Henry's six wives unfold here, including the birth of his son and heir.

*33. Henry VIII (detail), in a portrait after Hans Holbein. Despite his interest in building and his squirrel-like habit of collecting plate, jewellery and medals in the new Renaissance designs, the art that Henry loved most was music. He owned over 300 musical instruments at the time of his death and thirty-three of his own compositions have survived.*

*34. Anne Boleyn (c. 1500–1536), by an unknown artist, sixteenth century, after an original of c. 1533–36. The accusations against her of adultery were almost certainly false. Her 'crimes' were a failure to provide Henry with a male heir and her quarrel with the King's chief minister Thomas Cromwell.*

## Henry VIII (1509–1547) takes Hampton Court

When Cardinal Wolsey wrote to Henry VIII (fig. 33), he would address letters from "your majesty's house" at Hampton Court. The convention was to speak as if the King owned each one of his subjects' houses, and it was an honour to them if he chose to stay there. Henry had visited Hampton Court throughout the 1520s, but Wolsey finally lost his sure political touch when he opposed the King's divorce from his first wife, Catherine of Aragon, and fell foul of the King's new mistress, Anne Boleyn. In September 1528 Wolsey received a peremptory letter from Henry's treasurer ordering him to vacate Hampton Court in four days' time. Henry had decided to eject Wolsey and to make Hampton Court his own.

Wolsey's difficulties were caused by Henry's decision to divorce Catherine, who had failed to provide him with a son. The King intended to marry Anne Boleyn (fig. 34), the courtier with whom he had fallen in love. A court of legates from Rome met to judge the matter but failed to agree and the case was called back to the Pope. This incident led to Henry's decision to separate the Church of England from that of Rome, with himself at its head. The move had far-reaching consequences, not least the dissolution of England's monasteries and a massive redistribution of their wealth. Wolsey appeared powerless to obtain the divorce the King wanted, and this confirmed Anne Boleyn as his bitter enemy. Even before Wolsey's fall from favour, work had begun on the construction of "Anne Bouillayne's lodgynges at Hampton Courte".

When news finally arrived that the Pope had categorically forbidden Henry's remarriage, Wolsey was disgraced. On 4 November 1530 he was arrested; he then fell ill with what was reported as dysentery, and died on 29 November. When Wolsey's servant George Cavendish brought the news to Henry at Hampton

Catherine of Aragon's personal emblem was the pomegranate or 'Granada apple', a symbol of fertility. This was cruelly ironic in the light of the difficulty Catherine had in producing a son.

Anne of Cleves, Henry VIII's fourth wife, who was swiftly rejected by her husband, remained at court after their divorce. There she was known as 'the king's sister'.

When Henry VIII and Catherine Parr were married at Hampton Court in 1543, her vows included the unusual promise "... in sickness and in health, to be bonayre and buxome in bed and at board, till death us do part".

Court, he found the King practising archery in the park and not over-eager to hear the news. "I will make an end of my game", Henry said, "and then will I talk with you."

Henry had not been greatly interested in architecture for the first twenty years of his life, leaving the necessary improvements to his palaces in Wolsey's hands. But now, with growing personal passion, he began to create a palace for pleasure and retirement with his second wife, Anne Boleyn, and his third, Jane Seymour, who had been Anne's lady-in-waiting. Both Anne and Jane had lavish lodgings built at Hampton Court, but ironically neither of them was to live long enough to enjoy them. Anne Boleyn was beheaded on the grounds of treasonous infidelity, and Jane Seymour died shortly after she had successfully provided the King with a son and heir.

### Henry VIII begins to build

Henry's programme of work began on 2 January 1529. The first phase of building included the construction of the enormous offices needed for Henry's kitchen staff, a Council Chamber from which he now

36. *One of the two rooms in the kitchens called 'dressers', used for dressing, or putting the finishing touches to dishes just before they were taken up the stairs to diners waiting in the Great Hall.*

intended to rule the country and a tower of private rooms for himself.

*Kitchens and sanitation*
As many as 800 servants could accompany Henry on his visits to Hampton Court, and the kitchens he inherited from Lord Daubeney and Cardinal Wolsey were quite simply inadequate. In 1529–30, the capacity of the Great Kitchen to serve the meals eaten in the Great Hall was doubled and a second serving-place was added to the south, allowing twice as many waiters as before to carry food up to the Great Hall (fig. 35). The extended Great Kitchen now contained six fireplaces. To its west three new small courtyards sprang up, surrounded by many specialized offices for boiling, pastry-making, fruit and spices. Confectioners worked in an upstairs room, producing delicate sweets and comfits on chafing dishes. There were larders for fish, meat and grain. The whole kitchen complex contained fifty rooms and three cellars (fig. 36). Accounts were kept by the officers of the Greencloth, whose office lay over the outer gate to the kitchens so that they could monitor supplies coming into the palace.

In 1554, a Spanish visitor to the court of Mary I described her kitchens as "veritable hells, such is the stir and bustle in them ... . The usual daily consumption is eighty to one hundred sheep ... a dozen fat beeves, a dozen and a half calves, without mentioning poultry, game, deer, boars and great numbers of rabbits. There is plenty of beer here, and they drink more than would fill the Valladolid river." Given the number of people involved and the constrictions of space, it is not surprising that frequent royal commands were needed to reform abuses. On one occasion the kitchen boys were commanded not to "go naked or in garments of such vileness as they do now, and have been accustomed to do, nor lie in the nights and days in the kitchen or ground by the fireside".

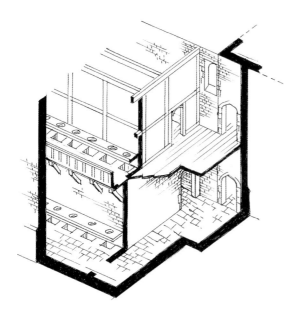

TOP LEFT *37. Chemical analysis of the contents of this chamberpot, excavated from the Tudor palace, shows that it still contains traces of urine.*

ABOVE *38. A plan of the communal toilet in the south-western part of the palace, reconstructed by Daphne Ford. In Elizabethan times this was known as 'The Great House of Easement'.*

TOP RIGHT *39. The 'Bayne Tower' was begun in April 1529 to provide Henry VIII with a new suite of private rooms. These contained the 'bayne' (a sixteenth-century word for bath) from which the tower takes its name.*

Drinking water was brought to Hampton Court by a remarkable network of underground brick conduits and lead pipes running all the way from a spring on Kingston Hill. The sanitary needs of the throngs of Tudor courtiers were met in a variety of ways (fig. 37). The lodgings of senior members of the court, such as those in Base Court, had their own garderobe shafts. Lower-ranking members of the court would use the 'common jakes' in the south-west corner of the palace (fig. 38), later known as the Great House of Easement, where lavatories drained via the moat into the river. Twenty-eight people could be seated here simultaneously.

### Rooms for the King

Henry's second project was the creation of a Council Chamber, built just to the north-west of the Chapel, and a suite of private rooms for himself named the Bayne Tower (fig. 39). This new three-storey tower of lodgings lay to the east of Clock Court and contained a first-floor bedroom and adjoining bathroom. A furnace in a room nearby heated water for his circular bathtub. The first floor also contained his Privy Closet, decorated with Italianate wall paintings by Toto del Nunziata and with built-in cupboards. In Henry's library on the floor above, his books were protected behind lockable glass doors, with curtains to prevent fading. The first-floor bedchamber was the last in the chain of increasingly important rooms that extended from the palace entrance, eventually leading – for those who were sufficiently exalted – right to the King's own presence.

With so many people swarming around at court, there was little chance of maintaining order without the senior officers: the Lord Chamberlain and the Groom of the Stool. These two divided the governance of the King's lodgings between them, the Lord Chamberlain being responsible for the outer rooms and the Groom of the Stool for the Privy Chamber and the private rooms beyond. Once Henry realized that these private or privy rooms were becoming less and less exclusive, he was motivated from 1537 to

create the set of 'secret' lodgings that overlooked the gardens, in roughly the same position as the later suite of royal apartments built for William III. Henry's new lodgings formed the southern side of a new court, known as Cloister Green Court, roughly mirroring the shape of Fountain Court, which replaced it over 150 years later.

## The Great Hall

In 1532 Henry rebuilt the Great Hall, the first in the sequence of rooms leading towards his private lodgings (fig. 40). It seems that Wolsey himself had begun rebuilding Lord Daubeney's hall; the oriel window, for example, is almost identical to that constructed by Wolsey's masons at his Oxford college, Christ Church. It is not quite clear how far Wolsey's work had advanced, but this oriel window now became part of a dramatically improved Great Hall.

Henry's designers, Christopher Dickenson and James Nedeham, sat down to work in their tracing houses. The roof of the Great Hall is of hammer-beam construction. This design traditionally allowed carpenters to span halls of a greater width than the longest available timbers. However, timbers 12 m (40 ft) in length, the width of the hall at Hampton Court, were readily available. The hammerbeam design, echoing the roof of Westminster Hall, was deliberately chosen to symbolize royalty, antiquity and chivalry. A stone hearth lay in the centre of the hall and smoke was intended to escape through a shuttered louvre above it in the medieval fashion. Yet the absence of any soot on the timbers of the louvre itself throws doubt upon whether this archaic feature was ever used. The roof was decorated with carved and painted heads, and badges celebrating the King and Queen. The carved screen that remains today was erected across the 'lower' or entrance end of the hall, supporting a gallery for musicians above, while a dais was constructed at the other, 'higher' end.

As part of the rebuilding of the hall, a new processional staircase provided access from the gatehouse between Base and Clock Courts up to the first-floor level containing the hall and the King's lodgings. This entrance is called Anne Boleyn's Gateway today, and a new stone vault was constructed within it decorated with the initials of Anne Boleyn and Henry (fig. 41). (It was replaced in the nineteenth century with a copy of the original.) Anne's badges and initials also appear next to Henry's beneath the royal coats of arms decorating the hall's roof. This was the busiest period of Henry's ten-year building programme at Hampton Court: 208 labourers, 45 carpenters, 70 masons and 81 bricklayers were employed at the palace in 1535.

## The palace of pleasure

Henry and Anne would regularly visit Hampton Court to inspect the progress of work and perhaps to enjoy some of the palace's amenities, which in due course would include extensive gardens, a tiltyard, archery butts in the park, bowling alleys (and a workshop for the turner who made the King's bowling balls). Both outdoor and indoor tennis plays lay to the north-east of the palace (fig. 42). The Venetian ambassador described how Henry was "most fond of tennis, at which game it is the prettiest thing in the world to see his play, his fair skin glowing through a shirt of the finest texture".

To the south of the palace lay Henry's Privy Garden. Here heraldic beasts were mounted on poles, trellis fences created compartments within which plants were arranged in simple knot patterns, and a banqueting house with an onion-shaped domed roof stood atop a mound. Down by the river, a large brick building, later known as the Water Gallery, was constructed upon piles (fig. 43). This provided both a convenient place for landing by boat and magnificent views of the gardens and palace. The fishponds in the neighbouring section of the gardens were kept full by the efforts of labourers who were paid for "ladling of water out of the Thames to fill the ponds in the night times".

Hampton Court became a wonderful place for entertainment and pleasure. In 1537 a dazzling display of the King's gold and silver plate was set up in the banqueting house on the mound to impress onlookers; a path lined with rosemary spiralled up to the building's entrance. Sir Thomas Cawarden's account books for 1546 record the construction of a further two temporary banqueting houses in the park. Made of waxed canvas with horn windows, they were intended for the reception of French visitors after the signing of a peace treaty. Henry also began to create a 4000-ha (10,000-acre) chase, or private hunting ground, by seizing and fencing the surrounding land. The hunting available at Hampton Court was a considerable part of its appeal to the King, a keen huntsman, as were many of his successors.

## Lodgings for Henry's queens

Catherine of Aragon had stayed in the suite of rooms built by Wolsey on the east side of Clock Court. Anne Boleyn had rooms at Hampton Court from 1529, but the old queen's residence was not good enough. Accordingly, in 1533 a grander suite of apartments was begun for her, forming the north and east sides of the new Cloister Green Court. Despite all this, in 1536 Anne fell from the King's favour. After giving birth to her daughter Elizabeth, and then miscarrying a boy, she was considered to have failed in her duty to provide the King with a male heir and an excuse was found to accuse her of adultery, a treasonable offence for a queen. Meanwhile, Henry had been seen "to affect Jane Seymour, and having her on his knee", which made Anne fear that he would cast her aside "like the late queen". Less than four months after the natural death of the repudiated

Queen Catherine, Anne Boleyn was found guilty of treason and bravely stepped on to the scaffold at the Tower of London, "as gay as if she was not going to die". That very night Jane Seymour and the King dined together, and their betrothal took place the next morning.

With the King's marriage to Jane in 1536, a new flurry of work at Hampton Court commenced; the badges and initials of Anne Boleyn were swiftly erased and replaced by those of Jane Seymour

(figs. 45, 46, 49). The craftsmen received overtime payments for "working in their own times and drinking times ... for the hasty expedition" of the bridge over the moat. Here the leopard (Anne's symbol) was swiftly converted into the panther of Jane Seymour (fig. 44). Soon Jane became pregnant and the King's impatience began to make itself felt. A great spurt of work was needed to provide bigger and better lodgings for the new Queen on the East Front. The lodgings so recently built for Anne Boleyn were now rebuilt for Jane. A further new set of lodgings for the prince that Jane was expected to provide was also begun on the north side of the palace. These contained a rocking room for the prince's cradle as well as his own Privy Kitchen. In October 1537 the future King Edward VI was born at Hampton Court. Not

quite two weeks later his mother died from complications following the birth, without ever having had the chance to take advantage of her new rooms and gallery looking east over the park.

Henry's fourth wife, the German princess Anne of Cleves, had little to do with Hampton Court; Henry, never satisfied with her physical appearance, soon divorced her. But the palace was the location of important scenes in the life of his penultimate wife, Catherine Howard (fig. 48). Henry's divorce from Anne of Cleves came through in July 1540. On 8 August Catherine Howard was married to Henry and, as the new Queen, sat next to him in the royal closet in the Chapel at Hampton Court. After making a progress round the country, they returned to Hampton Court on 24 October, and Henry was

RIGHT 45. *An extract from the Hampton Court accounts, recording payments to the gilders for changing vanes from Anne Boleyn's arms to Jane Seymour's in 1536.*

FAR RIGHT 46. *The arms of Jane Seymour on a fragment of stone shield excavated from the moat in 1909–10. The design incorporates a phoenix, a hawthorn tree and a gateway.*

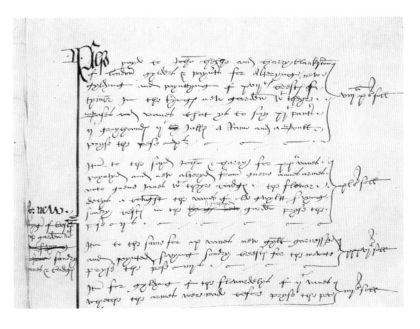

so happy that during Mass he gave "most hearty thanks for the good life he led and trusted to lead with his wife".

However, it was at Hampton Court little more than a year later that Catherine was first accused of the serious crimes that would lead to her being placed under house arrest and eventually condemned to death (fig. 50). Once again the accusation was adultery, a charge this time with more substance to it. Henry had been besotted with his new young wife and turned against her all the more viciously. She was accused of unchastity before she married the King, although it had been claimed that she came to him a virgin, but what sealed the Queen's fate was the rumour that during her marriage she had had an affair with Thomas Culpepper, one of Henry's Gentlemen of the Bedchamber.

The ghostly figure traditionally glimpsed in the Haunted Gallery (fig. 51) is supposed to be Catherine herself, running along it in a desperate effort to reach the King at Mass in order to plead her innocence. While there is no contemporary evidence for this, we do know that she was ordered to remain in her own rooms, and that although she was allowed to keep her key to pass between her rooms, from there she could not have reached the gallery she is said to haunt. Catherine's pleas to her husband were of no avail: she was accused of leading "an abominable, base, carnal, voluptuous, and vicious life, like a common harlot, with diverse persons" and was executed at the Tower of London on 13 February 1542.

## The Chapel Royal

On feast or holy days, the King would hear Mass from the Holyday Closet, a room overlooking the Chapel. On other days he was often keen to leave the palace early to reach the hunting field and would hear Mass at seven o'clock in his Privy Closet within

50. *The Great Watching Chamber. Late in 1541, the members of Catherine Howard's household were called to this room, told of the Queen's misdeeds, and dismissed from her service. At that time there would have been a wide Tudor fireplace and a brightly coloured heraldic frieze between the tops of the tapestries and the ceiling. In the eighteenth century the Great Watching Chamber was used as an ante-room to the theatre made in the Great Hall.*

his own lodgings, sometimes reading state papers throughout the service. On feast-days the King would process in a stately manner to the Chapel, as Wolsey had done, along what is today known as the Haunted Gallery. The most important procession took place at Epiphany, the twelfth day of Christmas, for which Henry would wear his crown and robes. The Holyday Closet and Chapel itself were now far superior to the simpler structure that Wolsey had built.

The Chapel, Henry's last great building project at the palace, was begun in 1535. The most important change was the addition of the fantastical ceiling, which still survives (fig. 54). The designer was probably William Clement, and its virtuosity clearly demonstrates his qualifications for his next task, which was to create another new palace for Henry not far from Hampton Court: the largely wooden structure of Nonsuch. Although little remains of Nonsuch Palace today, we can imagine its complexity and flamboyance from Hampton Court's Chapel

ceiling. Like the Great Hall roof, the ceiling has many decorative flourishes: trusses, vaults and pendants decorated with angels blasting their trumpets. The craftsmen John Hethe and Henry Blankston added colour and gilding.

At the same time, the Royal Pew was refitted to create the Holyday Closets at the west end of the Chapel. Previously there had been one large room for the King's use; now two were created, with a painted screen incorporating stained glass separating the King's private pew from the Queen's. Here it was that Henry first received the fateful news of Catherine Howard's adultery.

## Time and tide

One of the last additions that Henry made to the palace was the Astronomical Clock (fig. 52), which gives its name to Clock Court. Inscribed with the initials of its maker Nicholas Oursian and dated 1540, it has at its centre the earth with the sun revolving around it, while outer dials show the movements of

51. *The Haunted Gallery owes its name to the story of the desperate Catherine Howard, Henry VIII's fifth wife. In the late nineteenth century her ghost was described as "a female form, dressed in white". Residents living adjacent to the gallery reported "unearthly shriek[s]" in the dead of night, "followed immediately by perfect stillness".*

52. *The Astronomical Clock, made by Nicholas Oursian in 1540 to a design probably by Nicholas Kratzer, the astronomer described as 'Devisor of the King's Horologes'. Kratzer was paid fourpence a day in his post of Clock-keeper at Hampton Court.*

the moon and the number of days since the New Year. The clock's most cunning device was its ability to tell the time of high water at London Bridge, useful information at a time when tides governed travel to and from the palace.

After the death of Catherine Howard, the King aged rapidly, having "wonderfully felt the case of the queen". He grew increasingly fat – "His Highness waxed heavy with sickness, age and corpulence of the body" – and lost the use of his ulcerated legs. However, he soon returned to Hampton Court, where he entertained the ambassadors from the Holy Roman Emperor Charles V, and on 12 July 1543 he married his sixth and last wife in the Queen's Closet there. Catherine Parr was a good mother to Henry's three children; she acted as his consort throughout six days of sumptuous entertainment for the French ambassador; she even outlived her husband. Henry, the once handsome prince who had impressed Europe with his youthful agility, his brains and his looks, departed from Hampton Court for the last time in 1546, a sick old man, and died at Whitehall Palace in 1547.

53. *Henry VIII's Hampton Court as it would have appeared in 1547, in a reconstruction by Daphne Ford. Some areas of the building are shown schematically because of the lack of evidence. Detail is provided for the areas that either survive today or are shown in historic views of the palace.*

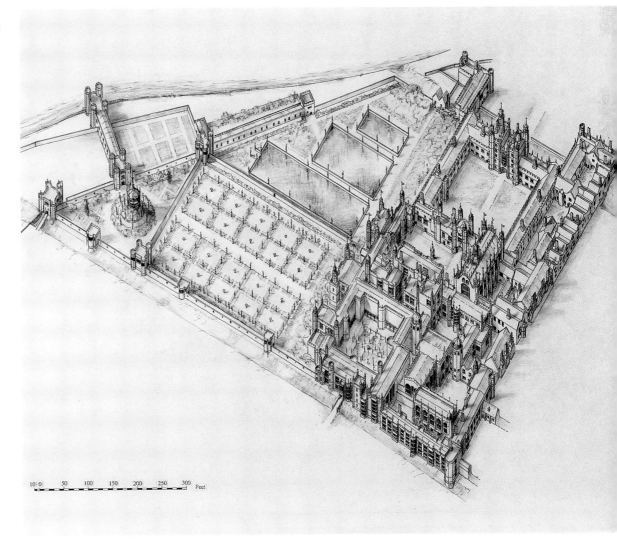

10 0   50   100   150   200   250   300   Feet

54. The ceiling of the Chapel Royal was installed for Henry VIII in 1535–36. The ceiling's components were carved at Sonning, several miles further up the River Thames, before being transported to Hampton Court and reassembled there.

# *The* LATER Tudors at *Hampton* COURT Palace 1547–1603

Edward VI and his half-sisters Mary I and Elizabeth I make few changes to their father's magnificent palace. Hampton Court is the scene of some important events in their lives, including a birth, a birth that never happened and several brushes with death.

*55. Edward VI, from the studio of William Scrots, c. 1546. Aged nine at his accession, Edward experienced both fun and fear during time spent at Hampton Court. A constant companion of the young King was Barnaby FitzPatrick, with whom he shared his lessons. Barnaby was Edward's whipping boy – whether Barnaby or Edward misbehaved, it was always Barnaby who was chastised.*

### Edward VI (1547–1553)

Edward VI (fig. 55), born at Hampton Court Palace on 12 October 1537, entered the world in a bedchamber in the old queen's lodgings high up on the second floor of the east side of Clock Court. The new suite planned for his mother, Jane Seymour, was not completed in time. Jane did, however, benefit from new curtains and a new bed for the lying-in ceremony. It would turn out to be her deathbed only twelve days later.

With Edward's birth, Henry VIII's ambition to found a dynasty was achieved at last. A triumphant christening procession, one of the great set-piece occasions of the splendid Tudor court, was planned (fig. 56). On 15 October the procession began at the Prince's brand-new lodgings north of Chapel Court and passed through the adjacent Council Chamber before snaking around the palace and back along the

cloisters until finally arriving at the Chapel. Eighty knights, gentlemen and squires led the way, carrying wax torches that were to remain unlit until after the ceremony. The baby was carried by a bevy of further noblemen and women, with the train of his robe carefully fanned out behind him and a rich canopy lifted above him by four Gentlemen of the King's Privy Chamber.

Edward's life was to be regrettably short. Henry died when Edward was nine years old and the young Prince was placed under the care of his uncle, Jane's brother the Duke of Somerset, who declared himself the King's Protector. Hampton Court was a place that the boy King visited relatively frequently, often with his attendant gentlemen, to play games on horseback in the park or the Tiltyard. Somerset's annexation of the young King was not well received by other factions of nobles, and news came of an

*56. Part of the christening procession of Prince Edward, later Edward VI, in 1537. The baby Prince is carried beneath a canopy borne by gentlemen of the household. His elder half-sister, the Princess Mary, follows him, with a lady-in-waiting carrying her train.*

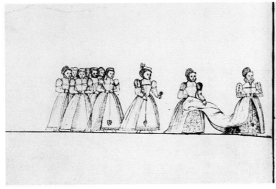

Mary I was loved by her entourage but disliked by the nation. She stayed only in her Thames-side palaces between Whitehall and Hampton Court.

In 1554, Philip II of Spain hid himself behind a tapestry at Hampton Court in order to eavesdrop on his Catholic wife Mary I's interrogation of her Protestant half-sister Elizabeth.

When in 1564 Elizabeth I quizzed Sir James Melville, visiting from the court of her rival, Mary Queen of Scots, he admitted reluctantly that she, Elizabeth, was the better dancer.

attack planned to be mounted on Hampton Court to remove Edward from Somerset's influence. Armed men were drawn up and inspected in Base Court, but Somerset decided instead to flee with the King to the safer stronghold of Windsor. It was all in vain: Edward fell ill with broncho-pneumonia in February 1553 and died on 6 July at Greenwich, aged fifteen.

### Mary I (1553–1558)

Edward's "Device for the Succession", written on his deathbed, willed his crown to his Protestant cousin the Duchess of Suffolk. So it was that the Duchess's daughter, Lady Jane Grey, became queen for nine days before being deposed and executed by Edward's Catholic half-sister Mary, who as Henry VIII's eldest child had a much stronger blood claim to the crown.

The five years of Mary's reign were dangerous ones for England's Protestants, above all for the Queen's half-sister Elizabeth. The Princess was next in line to the throne but was vulnerable to being disinherited; she was accused of treason and even threatened with execution by Mary. Hampton Court Palace was the setting of many tense scenes.

In 1554 ambassadors arrived at Hampton Court to offer Mary the hand of King Philip II of Spain in marriage. After the Queen's ritual show of reluctance, she was pleased and seems to have become truly fond of her Spanish husband, despite his heavy Habsburg looks and gloomy temperament. Shortly after their marriage the thirty-eight-year-old Mary convinced herself that she was pregnant and in April 1555 the ladies of the court gathered at Hampton Court for the birth. Princess Elizabeth was brought to the palace and kept under close arrest – "the doors being shut on her, the soldiers in their ancient posture of watch and guard" – for fear that she would foment Protestant rebellion. On St George's Day Philip heard Mass in the Chapel, then led a procession of the Knights of the Garter around the cloisters and courts. Mary peered down through her chamber window, so "that hundreds did see her", in order to dispel rumours of her death.

Mary never gave birth; hers turned out to be a false pregnancy. In 1557 her husband returned to Spain and Mary was left alone and childless, having contracted cancer of the stomach, which killed her in November 1558. Less than a week later the twenty-five-year-old Queen Elizabeth, Anne Boleyn's daughter, entered London in triumph.

## Elizabeth I (1558–1603)

### Improvements to the palace

When Queen Elizabeth visited Hampton Court Palace she used her father's lodgings. Elizabeth concentrated her building works on Whitehall Palace, continuing Henry VIII's work there, but as early as 1559 her Lord Treasurer drew up a list of works required at Hampton Court. Although nothing would be done quickly, he wrote that he had "found a new place for a privy kitchen and all offices to it" with the advantage that "the trouble of the old privy kitchen and the sewers of all evil savours from the same shall be clearly taken away". This referred to the private kitchen where Henry VIII's own meals were cooked. In 1570 Elizabeth's new Privy Kitchen was built, and still stands, to the east of Daubeney's kitchen.

In 1559 the Lord Treasurer proposed to "take away all the sight of every chamber that has his light into the pond gardens, saving only [Elizabeth's] own lights". By blocking these windows, "her majesty shall walk secretly all hours and times without looking upon her out of any place". On cold mornings Elizabeth liked to march about vigorously in the heraldic gardens laid out by her father. Only if onlookers approached would she adopt a slower and more regal pace. Elizabeth appointed the Frenchman John Markye to carry out improvements to the gardens, replacing the many elaborate compartments with larger divisions in which the Queen's badges were set out in coloured gravel. His assistants included an interpreter.

### Sickness and pleasure

Elizabeth had returned to Hampton Court as queen nine months into her reign (fig. 58). She was at the palace once again in October 1562, when she nearly lost her life. She was so ill with smallpox that her doctors thought she could not possibly recover, but by the end of the month the indomitable Queen was out of bed, and "attending to the marks of her face to avoid disfigurement". However, in the same year the disease caused the death of Sibell Penn, a lady of Elizabeth's bedchamber and Edward VI's

58. *Elizabeth I receiving Dutch emissaries, c. 1585, in a room that shows how Hampton Court might have been furnished during ambassadors' visits. Elizabeth is shown rising from her chair beneath her red Cloth of Estate while the foreign visitors kneel before her on the matting.*

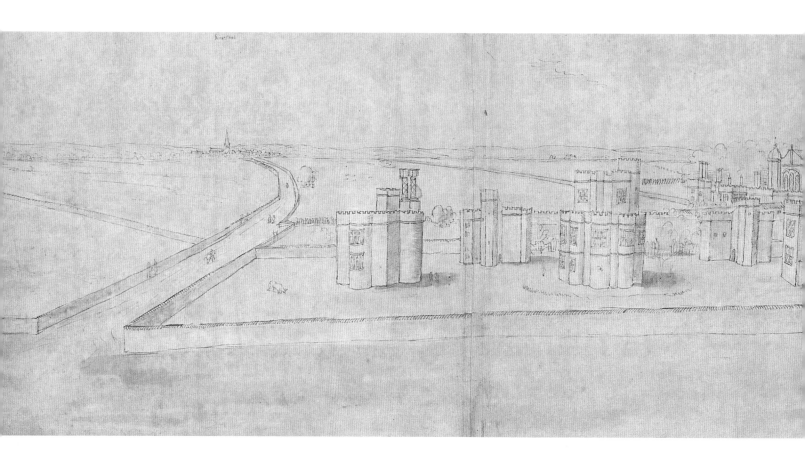

59. *Anthonis van den Wyngaerde's view of Hampton Court from the north, c. 1558–62. To the left are the towers for spectators of the tilt, only one of which survives today. The Great Hall rises from a mass of turrets in the centre of the view and to its right lies the enormous Great Gatehouse at its original full height.*

60. *Natives from Sir Walter Ralegh's ill-fated Roanoke colony in North America were among the most exotic visitors to the court of Elizabeth I. This watercolour of a shaman from the Roanoke people was painted by John White, the colony's governor.*

former dry-nurse. Mrs Penn's death gives rise to one of the most persistent ghost stories of the palace: her unquiet spirit is said to have been heard revolving a spinning-wheel in a room in the palace after her tomb in Hampton parish church was disturbed in 1829.

After her bout of smallpox, Elizabeth kept away from Hampton Court for five years. Only from 1567 did it once again become a regular autumn or winter residence. The palace's entertainments included tilting or jousting, especially on the anniversary of the Queen's Accession Day. Henry VIII's viewing towers overlooking the lists in the Tiltyard (fig. 59) were probably never used in his day but in 1569 they housed spectators at the first tournament of Elizabeth's reign to be held at Hampton Court. Between tournaments, the towers provided lodgings for members of the court; four gentlemen lost all their belongings when a thief broke into one tower in 1594.

At Christmas and New Year, the Great Hall of the palace was transformed into a 'masking house' or indoor theatre and became the setting for masques and plays. A stage was erected, the Great Watching Chamber was used for rehearsals and the pantry behind the screens passage became the 'tiring', attiring or dressing room for the actors. The painted canvas backdrops included representations of "seven cities, one village, and one country house".

The marvels of Elizabeth's palace included the fabulous room to the south-east called 'Paradise'.

Built by Henry VIII, it was now refurbished with a new painted ceiling and decorated with precious metals and gems. Visitors found that "everything glitters so with silver, gold and jewels, as to dazzle one's eyes, there is a musical instrument made all of glass except the strings". Here the Queen entertained her most distinguished guests and her greatest favourites. Among those favourites was Sir Walter Ralegh, who brought with him in October 1584 some of the strangest visitors the royal palace had ever seen, the first two Native Americans to come to England from his New World colony at Roanoke in Virginia (fig. 60). Lupold von Wedel, a traveller who spent almost a year at court (but rarely even glimpsed the Queen in that time) was as much amazed as any other courtier. "They wear no shirts," he wrote, "only a piece of fur to cover the pudenda and the skins of wild animals to cover their shoulders", although to meet the Queen, for modesty, "they are clad in brown taffeta".

One of the last improvements to Elizabeth's palace, between 1584 and 1591, was a replacement for her father's great fountain in what is now Clock Court. The earlier Gothic fountain may well have been made of wood and, therefore, probably rotted away. The new design was octagonal, decorated with restrained classical arches and pillars, and contained a secret device that could "make water play upon the ladies and others who are standing by, and give them a thorough wetting".

With this characteristic piece of Tudor trickery, Elizabeth's improvements to the palace were complete. She departed from Hampton Court for the last time in 1599, stubbornly insisting on mounting a horse against the advice of her servants. As she passed through Kingston, one old man fell on his knees and prayed that "she might live a hundred years". This pleased the Queen, but she had only four years left to live and died at Richmond Palace on 24 March 1603.

# SEVENTEENTH-Century *Hampton* COURT Palace 1603–89

The seventeenth-century Stuart kings look after Hampton Court carefully, making some small but highly significant improvements. The palace remains an important place for entertainment, hunting and honeymoons, although it is also used as a royal prison during the Civil War.

61. *Gerard van Honthorst, Mercury Presenting the Liberal Arts to Apollo and Diana (detail), 1628. Charles I and Henrietta Maria, leaning down from their cloud to the left, are depicted as Apollo and Diana. The Duke of Buckingham below them is Mercury in his winged cap. The whole painting captures the atmosphere and costumes of a masque, telling the story of how the Liberal Arts were driven out of Italy by "barbarous Goths and Vandals" but found a home in Britain, "this happy island". Masques and allegory were an important component of life and entertainment at the early Stuart court.*

62. *James I after John de Critz the Elder, c. 1606. The only son of Mary Queen of Scots, James was a successful king of Scotland and was invited to take the English throne as well after Elizabeth I's death in 1603. He was witty and scholarly, although sometimes brutally frank to those who opposed him on religious issues. He responded to one critical sermon in 1585 with the words "I will not give a turd for thy preaching."*

## James I (1603–1625)

A new king and a new dynasty as well as a new century arrived with the accession of Elizabeth's Scottish cousin to the throne of England in 1603 (fig. 62). The Protestant James VI of Scots, son of the Catholic Mary Queen of Scots who had been the focus of many plots against Elizabeth, came to London with a new band of courtiers and a new style of culture and entertainment.

Bubonic plague in London had driven the court to celebrate the first Christmas and New Year of James's reign at Hampton Court. "The Queene intendeth to make a mask this Christmas", announced the King's cousin Arbella Stuart in a letter written from the palace (fig. 61), and permission was given for the late Queen Elizabeth's wardrobe at the Tower of London to be raided for costumes (fig. 63). A new dais was built in the Great Hall to accommodate the King and Queen and the ambassadors from foreign courts who would be invited to watch the spectacles of the season. One of these was Samuel Daniels's masque *The Vision of the Twelve Goddesses*. His stage directions record how the Queen herself took "the part of Pallas, in a blue mantle, with a silver embroidery of all weapons and engines of war, with a helmet-dressing on her head". She descended by a winding stair from a "paradisical mountain" constructed at the lower end of the hall to perform a dance before the King seated beneath his Cloth of Estate (fig. 64). All the ambassadors and courtiers joined in the dancing,

and young Prince Henry was thrown between them "like a tennis ball".

James I has always had an unfortunate reputation. One hostile but influential observer, writing much later, described how the new King was "of middle stature, more corpulent through his clothes than his body" (he wore padded doublets to protect him from

As Hampton Court was sufficiently distant from London to be safe, it was a convenient refuge when bubonic plague raged. Outbreaks occurred in 1592, 1603, 1625, 1636 and finally in 1665.

Jeffrey Hudson (1619–82) was the pet dwarf at the court of Charles I and Henrietta Maria. He went into royal service aged eight, when he was eighteen inches (46 cm) tall.

Listed in the 1649 inventory of "the late King's goods" was Henry VIII's crown. This was melted down by the Parliamentarians with the rest of the regalia.

an assassin's dagger). His eyes were "large, ever rolling after any stranger that came in his presence". His tongue was "too large for his mouth, which ever made him speak full in the mouth and made him drink very uncomely". This well-known but unkind pen-portrait masks a bisexual, intelligent and disputatious monarch, whose time at Hampton Court was characterized by his love of literature as well as of lavish entertainment.

The early Stuart court was notorious for the inventiveness both of its masques and of its debauchery. Performances were followed by a rush to the supper table in the King's Presence Chamber, where food and drink were seized with "accustomed confusion". Visits from the Danish family of James's wife Anne were particularly riotous. Sir John Harington blamed the Danes for the heavy drinking habits that the court adopted: "The Dane hath strangely wrought on our good English nobles; for those whom I could never get to taste good liquor, now follow the fashion, and wallow in beastly delights. The ladies abandon their sobriety and are seen to roll about in intoxication."

Yet Hampton Court was not all frivolity. The celebrations in the Great Hall for the New Year in 1604 included performances by the King's Men, whose resident dramatist was William Shakespeare. Later that same month came James I's great religious conference at Hampton Court. The King invited representatives of both the radical puritan movement and the more conformist members of the Church of England to discuss their differences over doctrinal issues such as the place of bishops and ritual in worship. The meeting led to the decision to publish an authorized translation of the Bible into English, the King James Bible. The puritans were led by Laurence Chaderton, Master of Emmanuel College, Cambridge. They may have been overwhelmed and intimidated both by their summons into the Privy Chamber of Henry VIII's palace, where "kneeling, they made their case to the King, who was seated with the young Prince Henry on a stool at his side", and by the King's disregard for their arguments. James I loved theological debate and joined in himself, though Sir John Harington recorded that "the King talked much Latin, and disputed with Dr Reynolds [a puritan]; but he rather used upbraidings than arguments; and told them they wanted to strip Christ again, and bid them *away with their snivelling*".

James's other great passion – apart from young men such as his favourites Robert Carr, Earl of Somerset, and George Villiers, Duke of Buckingham – was the hunt. He restocked the park and Hampton Court became a useful base for his sport. In September 1609 James issued a proclamation from the palace "against hunters, stealers, and killers of deer,

within any of the king's majesties forests, chases or parks". He also fulminated against the "bold and barbarous insolency of multitudes of vulgar people who, pressing upon us in our sports as we are hunting, do ride over our dogs, break their backs, spoil our game" and "run over and destroy the corn". Some of the wooden stags' heads mounted with antlers that remain in the Great Hall and Horn Room date from Stuart times (fig. 65). The palace's collection of horns, later described by John Evelyn as "vast beams of stags, elks, antelopes etc.", also came to include the fossilized horns of an Irish elk, excavated from a bog in County Clare and presented to Charles II in 1684.

Under James I, Hampton Court benefited from a low but constant level of expenditure on maintenance. The Great Hall was repaired in 1614, the Astronomical Clock was repainted in 1619 and the ceiling of the Paradise Chamber also underwent a lengthy programme of restoration. The royal court fell into the pattern of an annual autumnal visit to the palace, but it was home for longer periods to James's eldest son

Prince Henry, who died on 6 November 1612, aged eighteen. The Prince's mother, Queen Anne, was at Hampton Court when she died in 1619. One of her ladies recorded how "we all stayed in the chamber next to her bedchamber till she sent a command to us to go to bed, and would not suffer us to watch that night". At the last, the Queen gave "five or six groans", but "had the pleasantest going out of this world that ever anybody had".

## Charles I (1625–1649)

At the time of his accession in 1625, Charles I was heavily influenced by his father's former favourite, the Duke of Buckingham. Charles's elder brother Prince Henry had died before he could succeed to the throne and the Duke now took a flattering interest in the shy and stuttering younger prince, seriously rivalling his new wife, the French princess Henrietta Maria, in the King's affections. Hampton Court became the setting for painful quarrels between Queen and King; one of the points at issue

66. *The tennis court, built in the reign of Charles I and remodelled in the reign of Charles II, is still in use today and is the venue for the British Open Real Tennis Championships. The game is played by bouncing the ball from the roofs of the penthouses surrounding the court as well as passing it over the net.*

was the Queen's large, French-speaking household. The French ambassador, arriving in England in the hope of making peace between the royal couple, paid a visit to Charles I at Hampton Court and was received in a gallery. Charles raged at his wife's refusal to embrace English ways, or even to learn the English language. To the ambassador's annoyance, the Duke of Buckingham interrupted this private audience. Both sides jealously monitored the protocol of ambassadors' visits. In 1635 Sir Henry Vane, Comptroller of the Household, reprimanded the porters for having allowed the French ambassador to drive through the Great Gatehouse. His coach should have been left at the gate, but the porters complained that "the ambassador had entered within so swift as they could not, though they would, hinder it".

Charles made several important additions to the palace. The first major improvement, carried out in the autumn of the first year of his reign, was the building of a new tennis court (fig. 66). Charles had been taught to play by John Webb, Master of the King's Tennis Plays. The rules of the game had changed since Henry VIII's time. His open tennis play, on the same site as the later Royal Tennis Court, which still exists today, was replaced in stone. It was also during Charles's reign that the Longford River was created. This canalized river, which cost

over £4,000 to build in 1638–39, still brings water from 18 km (11 miles) away to power the fountains of the palace gardens. The Tudor conduits providing drinking water from a spring on Kingston Hill were overhauled at the same time. Henry VIII's heraldic Privy Garden was replaced by a simpler layout of four quarters in lawn. The gardens were now beautified with pieces from Charles's collection of statues and in 1625 a new "Horozontal dyall" (or sundial) was mounted on a stone pillar.

Charles I was probably the greatest art collector among all the English monarchs. His appetite for collecting was vast. At Hampton Court he arranged and maintained the contents of the palace according to old-fashioned principles. The inventory of his goods made for Parliament in 1649 after his execution shows that there were over 250 tapestries at Hampton Court. Comparison with Henry VIII's inventory of 1547 reveals that many of them had survived from the previous century. Far from having lost value, the late-Henrician set telling the story of Abraham (fig. 68) was now worth an astonishing £8,260. Elsewhere in the palace, Henry VIII's purple velvet canopy of state decorated with agates, chrysolites, garnets, sapphires and a large pearl was still in use, as were four great state beds from his day.

Living among these antique furnishings, Charles I selected appropriate paintings to complement them,

mainly portraits or religious subjects. His most striking new addition was Andrea Mantegna's series of the *Triumphs of Caesar* (fig. 67), purchased from the Gonzaga family in Mantua together with many other paintings from their celebrated collection. The *Triumphs* paintings arrived in England in 1630 and were installed in the Tudor long gallery. Calico curtains protected them from the light; today they may still be seen in darkened conditions in the converted Lower Orangery.

## The Civil War and Commonwealth (1649–1660)

From the 1630s onwards Charles I found himself in a difficult position: he needed large sums of money regularly voted to him but had been unable to convince the Lords and Commons that he deserved them, and so ruled without summoning Parliament. Relations between king and country deteriorated. Both sides eventually resorted to arms, and in 1643 the Parliamentarian forces seized Hampton Court. Motivated by the radical puritanism that sought to strip the Church of its frivolous trappings, they removed all the fine fittings from the Chapel: "the Altar was taken down … the Rails pulled down, and

TOP 67. *Andrea Mantegna, the* Triumphs of Caesar, *Canvas II: 'Bearers of statues of gods, of an image of a captured city, siege engines, inscribed tablets and trophies'. The* Triumphs of Caesar *paintings were considered important enough to be kept behind when most of the contents of Hampton Court were put up for sale during the Commonwealth.*

ABOVE 68. *'The Circumcision of Isaac' from* The History of Abraham *series of tapestries, c. 1545. Purchased for Henry VIII and probably intended for the Great Hall, the set of tapestries telling the story of Abraham remained in the Stuart palace. At the time of the Commonwealth they were given a higher valuation than any other work of art in Charles I's collection, but were reserved for Cromwell's use. The story of the birth of Isaac, heir to the aged Abraham, had both personal and dynastic significance for Henry VIII.*

the steps levelled; and the Popish pictures and superstitious Images that were in the glass windows were also demolished". Only the elaborate ceiling remained above a white-painted room for preaching, with twelve long hard forms laid out for the congregation.

By 1647, Charles I had lost a series of vital battles against the Parliamentarians and Hampton Court was selected as the captured King's prison. Oliver Cromwell, leader of the opposing forces, permitted the King to lead an elegant and comfortable life at the palace, more "as a guarded and attended prince than as a conquered and purchased captive". During his imprisonment, Charles was allowed visitors, including his children – he "was overjoyed to see them so well in health" – and the loyal John Evelyn, who kissed the King's hand and described his captors as "execrable villains". Even Cromwell paid visits to the King, in the hope of reaching some kind of compromise. He would regret the laxity of the prisoner's regime when in November Charles managed to escape.

Colonel Whalley, who had been in charge of security, later recounted how Charles outwitted him. The King's attendants told Whalley that their master was writing letters in his bedchamber. "I waited there without mistrust till six of the clock; then I began to doubt, and told the bed-chambermen, Mr Maule and Mr Murray, I wondered the king was so long a-writing." Growing increasingly suspicious, Whalley "lookt oft in at the key hole to see whether [he] could perceive his majesty, but could not". At eight o'clock, Whalley demanded access through the Privy Garden to the Privy Stairs, and found the bedchamber empty. A search revealed that the King was gone; he had escaped across the garden and was carried away by boat. His freedom was short-lived. Within two years he would be recaptured and executed before his own palace of Whitehall.

The next snapshot of Hampton Court comes in the 1649 survey of the house and estate made by the Parliamentary Commissioners who were responsible for the fate of the palace. The park was split into lots to be sold, but eventually it was decided that Oliver Cromwell, the leader of the newly founded Commonwealth, would himself require a country house. While some items from its furnishings were

retained for the Commonwealth's use, many items were lost or sold. A visitor in 1652 reported that the only tapestries left at Hampton Court were the ones "which had been behind the good ones to protect them from the damp of the walls".

By 1653, Cromwell had been made Lord Protector, reigning almost as a king. Whitehall was his principal residence but he spent most weekends at Hampton Court. "His custom", his biographer James Heath recorded, "was now to divert himself frequently at *Hampton Court* (which he had saved from Sale, with other Houses of the King's, for his own greatness), whither he went and came in post, with his Guards behind and before, as not yet secure of his Life from the justice of some avenging hand". He was right to be cautious: Charles I's son, now in exile, promised a reward to anyone who would assassinate Cromwell. In fact, after 1660 Captain Thomas Gardiner petitioned Charles II for money, which he claimed he deserved for his unsuccessful attempt on Cromwell's life with two loaded pistols and a dagger in one of the galleries at Hampton Court.

71. *The fountain of Arethusa (now known as Diana) in Bushy Park today. It was moved here from the Privy Garden in 1714.*

indelibly associated with the deposed Stuart régime. Cromwell's more puritanical supporters criticized him for having such titillating statues in the Privy Garden. "Demolish these monsters that are set up as ornaments", commanded one critic, Mrs Nethaway. Surrounded by her boys and dolphins, Arethusa stayed, although she would later be moved again, this time to Bushy Park, where she forms part of a grand eighteenth-century landscaping scheme (fig. 71). Renamed Diana, she stands above a fountain playing in the centre of the Round Pond.

Cromwell's daughter Mary was married at the palace and another daughter, Betty, died there. Meanwhile his wife, Elizabeth, earned a reputation as a parsimonious housekeeper in her supervision of the palace kitchens. After Cromwell's death in 1658, his son Richard attempted briefly and unsuccessfully to take up the reins of power. If there was to be a hereditary ruler, the country decided that it would prefer the house of Stuart, and Charles II was invited to return to his father's throne.

Witty as always, the cynical King asked the crowds of courtiers clustering round to welcome him home to Whitehall in 1660 why he had been in exile for so long, "for I see nobody that does not protest he has ever wished for my return". He was right in thinking that many preferred to forget their previous views in the face of the new Stuart reality.

## Charles II (1660–1685)

*The libertine King and his court*

Charles II was a frequent visitor to Hampton Court, first coming in the very month he was restored to the throne. The palace was the setting for some of the amorous adventures for which he is best known. He had been described as "Charles Stuart, a long dark man, about two yards high" in the Parliamentarians' 'wanted' posters during his escape from England after the Civil War (fig. 74). As he had spent so many years in the licentious court of France, he found himself criticized back in England for his easy relations with women and the attention he paid to their views. His household ordinances demanded a strict standard of behaviour that the King himself did not always match. "If any of Our Courte", read the rules

In some senses Cromwell did not act like a king. He commanded Sir Peter Lely to make his portrait "truly like me, and not flatter me at all; but remark all these roughnesses, pimples, warts and everything" (fig. 69). He kept open house at Hampton Court for the officers of the army, dining with them himself, when he would "disport himself, taking of his Drink freely, and opening himself every way to the most free familiarity". Yet this inspired soldier and religious extremist would adopt many of the trappings of the royal family that he had toppled. He moved into the former queen's apartments, overlooking the park on the east side of the palace, and even used her bed. His "Rich Bedchamber", for state rather than sleeping, was hung with five tapestries telling the story of Vulcan and Venus; his couch, two "elbow chairs" and four "back stools" were covered in "sky collour damaske".

Cromwell brought the delicate mythological figure of Arethusa from Somerset House to add to the central fountain of the Privy Garden; the statue was the work of Hubert Le Sueur, an artist who was

72. *Barbara Villiers, Countess of Castlemaine by Sir Peter Lely, c. 1665. Lely's series of beauties of the Stuart court, known as the 'Windsor Beauties', has often been thought to depict the King's mistresses, but in fact Barbara Villiers was the only one included. In 1663 it was said that she "commands the King as much as ever, and hath and doth what she will". She eventually lost her place as chief mistress to Louise de Kéroualle, Duchess of Portsmouth, in about 1671.*

governing life at Hampton Court, "shall be noysed to be a prophane person, an outrageous riotter, a ribald, a notorious drunkard, swearer, rayler, or quarrellor, a fugitive from his master, a bankrupt, suspected for a pilferer or a theefe, or be otherwise so vitious and unmannerly that he be unfit to live in vertuous and civill company, he shall be … admonished or punished as cause shall require."

One of the King's many mistresses, Barbara Villiers, Countess of Castlemaine, was installed at Hampton Court where she lived with her illegitimate children by him. She was given the lucrative office of Keeper and Chief Steward of the Mansion and Honour of Hampton Court. Lady Castlemaine is one of the beauties of Charles II's court painted by Sir Peter Lely in a series of portraits hanging today in the Communication Gallery (fig. 72). The idea for the portraits came from the King's sister-in-law Anne Hyde, Duchess of York, who was "desirous of the Pictures of the most handsome Persons about the Court", herself included.

The King's mistresses frequently presented Charles's wife, Catherine of Braganza, with a difficult situation, not least when she was expected to receive them at court. Catherine, not herself a great beauty, had come to England from Portugal in 1662. The artist and poet William Schellinks witnessed the preparations made for her honeymoon at Hampton Court, including the provision of a great green velvet bed topped with plumes. The Queen's lodgings were redecorated and a private Catholic oratory was set up for her. Wagons of provisions converged upon the palace and a forest of tents sprang up. In the crush, one of the King's choristers was run over by a cart and killed and one of the King's cooks drowned in the Thames. On 29 May, the King and his new Queen arrived by coach (see fig. 3). The aristocracy of England lined up to greet them. The new Queen walked through each room, acknowledging nobles of ever higher rank before finally reaching her own bedchamber on the East Front.

Money was a perennial problem for Charles II. On his return from exile he revived the hospitable custom of providing meals for the whole court, but the royal purse could not bear the expense. Outcry accompanied the abolition of free meals for lower courtiers in 1662. In 1664, the royal household's staff was reduced from 225 to 147. The Great Kitchens, no longer required for mass catering, began to be split up for individual courtiers' cooks, and the courtiers ate their meals in small groups in each other's lodgings. The Earl of Bedford made a five-day trip to Hampton Court for the purpose of hawking and hunting in 1670. He had to pay wages to his two grooms as well as charges for his own 'diet' or food. (At further expense, for the hawks' benefit, pigeons were transported from London to Hampton Court, and they were also tempted with 'hogs' hearts'.)

*Building and garden improvements*

Throughout the seventeenth century, Hampton Court had seen remarkably few changes or improvements. By and large, the Stuarts kept the palace as a monument to their Tudor forebears, "a relic of departed greatness" as the Venetian ambassador had remarked in 1653, putting what little energy they had into the garden layouts. Late seventeenth-century views on the palace, then nearly two centuries old, were not wholly positive, and John Evelyn pronounced it to be "as noble and uniform a pile, and as capacious, as any Gothic architecture can have made it".

However, Charles did make several significant improvements. One of these was the rebuilding of Charles I's tennis court to make the structure that still survives. Robert Long, the marker of the royal tennis courts, held his job for nine years from 1660; his tasks included providing shuttlecocks, lines and tennis shoes, and "attendance in supervising the workmen in his Majesty's Tennis Court at Hampton Court". The lines on the court were laid out in black marble, and the workmen were paid for the necessary building works. The King also spent his leisure hours on a new bowling green by the river, constructed in 1670. The Count of Grammont reported how "the turf is almost as smooth and level as the cloth of a billiard table. As soon as the heat of the day is over, the company assemble there: they play deep: and spectators are at liberty to make what bets they please."

The other major changes made by Charles II were the conversion of the old Tudor tennis court east of Chapel Court into lodgings for his brother, the Duke of York, and the construction of his own new lodgings in the south-east corner of the palace. This brand-new building (fig. 73), described as "Next Paradise" because of its proximity to the Tudor Paradise Chamber, had only a short life, as it was to be demolished in the next reign. Constructed in rubbed red brick, it provided a neat block of modern lodgings for Charles while at the same time being fully accessible from the first-floor Tudor king's suite. In 1675 the boards across the opening from Henry VIII's lodgings into the new rooms were removed, and the King slept in his new block while staying at Hampton Court for council meetings that summer.

These new rooms faced east towards the park, where Charles II's improvements were even more striking. The French designer André Mollet was commissioned to plant an avenue in preparation for the arrival of Catherine of Braganza. The magnificent Long Water Canal was cut through the park and 758 Dutch limes were planted in avenues along its flanks. John Evelyn, visiting in 1662, described

73. *Detail from an anonymous painting of the East Front of Hampton Court, c. 1680, showing the 'Building next Paradise'. Charles II's new lodging contained his closet and bedchamber. Both rooms were decorated with carved cornucopias over their fireplaces.*

how "the park, formerly a flat naked piece of Ground" was "now planted with sweete rows of lime-trees, and the canale for water now neere perfected". Other visitors, such as William Schellinks, described how one could glide "by water with the barges right up to the gardens".

## James II (1685–1688)

Charles II's canal and avenue would be very important in determining the layout of Hampton Court when it was extensively rebuilt in the 1690s. That would take place after England had deposed its king for the second time in the seventeenth century.

OPPOSITE 74. *Charles II by John Michael Wright, c. 1661. Although many of the changes to the palace building made by him or the Countess of Castlemaine, his former mistress, were swept away before the end of the century, Charles II left an enduring mark in the form of the park landscape.*

Charles's Catholic brother, James, Duke of York, had been the focus of bitter political fighting in an attempt to exclude him from the succession to the throne. Loyal London apprentices had even made their way out to Hampton Court in June 1681 to deliver a petition with 18,000 signatures supporting his right to succeed. The Duke's supporters won, and in 1685 he ascended the throne as James II. Within three years he had alienated most support and was to be driven from that throne in favour of a new Protestant king and queen, his son-in-law and daughter William III and Mary II, ruling as joint monarchs. Under them, the palace would be transformed.

# THE BAROQUE PALACE

# *William* and Mary's *Hampton* COURT Palace 1689–1702

England's new Protestant king and queen choose Hampton Court as their chief country residence and embark upon a great rebuilding programme. The Tudor lodgings are replaced with the grandeur of the Baroque palace, although Mary dies before the work is finished.

75. *Mary II by Sir Peter Lely, 1677. Mary loved her husband William though she was frequently parted from him by his need to travel and campaign. In 1678 she wrote sadly to a friend, "what can be more cruall in the world then parting with what on[e] loves?" Mary was industrious, sensible and more sociable than her husband. Her ladies and sometimes Mary herself spent part of the day "employed at their needles"; one of their number would "read to them while they were at work either Divinity or some profitable History".*

76. *William III (detail) by Sir Godfrey Kneller, c. 1690. Contemporary gossip and tales put about by William's Jacobite enemies claimed that despite the King's successful marriage he had sexual liaisons with two of his favourites, the Earl of Portland and later the Earl of Albemarle. This remains unproven, although William often stayed up late talking with his current favourite and the Earl of Albemarle's apartment at Hampton Court did connect with his own.*

## William III (1689–1702) and Mary II (1689–1694) become King and Queen of England

William of Orange (fig. 76) was a grandson of Charles I. In 1672 he followed the Orange family's tradition of becoming the civil and military leader, or Stadholder, of the Dutch Republic. His arranged marriage to his fifteen-year-old English cousin Mary (fig. 75), also a grandchild of Charles I and the daughter of James, Duke of York (later James II), took place five years later. When Mary heard the news of her impending wedding, she "wept all that afternoon and all the following day". William took his new bride back to the Dutch Republic, where she had to learn the language as well as familiarizing herself with the Orange family's homes: the Renaissance-style Honselaarsdijk, the secluded 'House in the Wood' outside The Hague, and later Het Loo, the country house that William bought and transformed into a private palace.

By 1688, the autocratic and Catholic James II had become increasingly mistrusted and his position as monarch was under threat. While James doubted that his own daughter, though Protestant, would plot against him – "you will be still as good a daughter to a father that has always loved you so tenderly", he told her – William made preparations to invade England. His fleet landed on 5 November 1688. On 13 February 1689, in the Banqueting House within Whitehall Palace, William and Mary were offered the Crown in the presence of the assembled Lords and Commons,

"whereupon there were loud shouts for Joy both in the Banqueting House and in all the Courts of Whitehall".

On 2 March the new King and Queen visited Hampton Court Palace. In the midst of political turmoil, it is astonishing that they were able to devote so much time and effort to buildings. In July news of a Catholic plot to depose William actually interrupted celebrations for the birth of a son to his sister-in-law,

LEFT In 1689 work began on the new southern range of the palace. Some of the workmen left for posterity graffiti and handprints in concealed areas of plaster.

RIGHT As a symbol of his importance at court, the Groom of the Stool wore the key to the Royal Bedchamber on a blue ribbon round his neck.

The locks in William III's downstairs bedchamber were positioned on the inside of the room's three doors so that William could make himself secure while he slept.

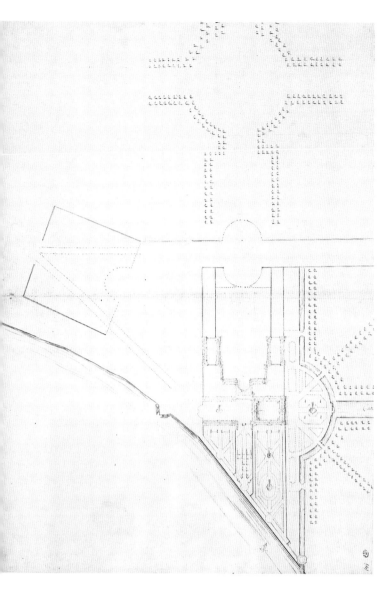

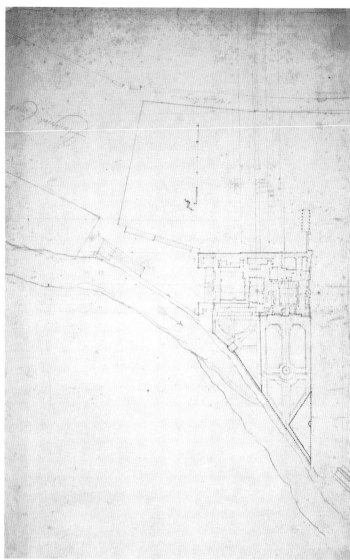

the future Queen Anne, at Hampton Court. But the old Tudor palace, despite its being "so very old built and so irregular", had many advantages as a home for this royal pair. Its clean air helped William's asthma, leading to his resolve "to live the greatest part of the year there". This decision to relocate was not universally popular; those involved in government found that "the King's inaccessibleness and living so at Hampton Court altogether" made it difficult to get business done. Ultimately this led to the royal couple's acquisition of the Earl of Nottingham's house in Kensington, then west of London, extending it to form the semi-metropolitan Kensington Palace.

## Plans for rebuilding Hampton Court

No sooner had William and Mary visited Hampton Court than they began to plan improvements. By 4 May their architect, Sir Christopher Wren, presented them with an estimate of the building costs, which meant that the many different schemes documented in the designs produced by Wren's office had been judged, revised and finally accepted. Wren,

Surveyor of the Royal Works, was a true polymath, a successful scientist before he turned to architecture. He had long wanted to build a royal palace, and found in Queen Mary a particularly sympathetic patron. Yet the project would bring him trouble and humiliation; eventually he would even find himself ousted by his rival, William Talman.

The royal couple and Wren did not begin with a blank piece of paper. The Tudor palace already stood in a mature landscape and Charles II's Long Water Canal would form the obvious axis of the East Front of the new palace. Their initial thinking was radical: to demolish nearly all of the Tudor palace, retaining only Henry VIII's Great Hall at the centre of a grand Baroque entrance facing north (fig. 77). Double avenues marching south across Bushy Park would culminate in a vast semicircular courtyard built around the Great Hall. The green-fingered Earl of Portland, the Superintendent of the King's Gardens with the power "to oversee and direct any plantations and works therein", began to plant the avenues, and they remain today.

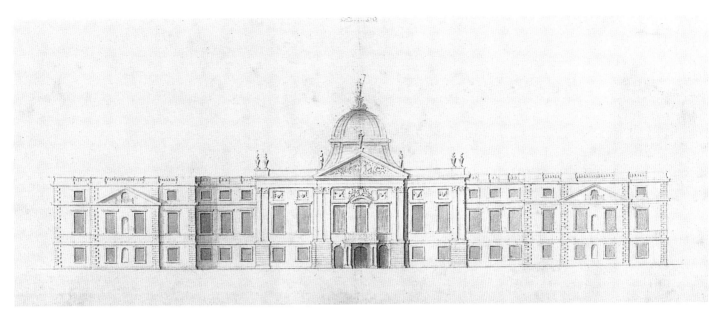

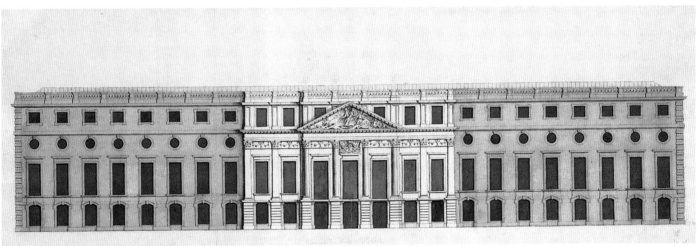

A variety of designs was now mooted in a flood of drawings from the Office of Works, but no single drawing appears to be in Wren's hand. This raises an important question: did Wren really design William and Mary's palace? Or was it more the work of others in his office, such as the talented Nicholas Hawksmoor? The probable answer is that while Wren employed several assistants – among them Hawksmoor in the case of Hampton Court – he himself provided the guiding inspiration behind their designs.

Yet the first scheme, and subsequent variations upon it, would never be built. It quickly became apparent that such a huge project would be difficult to finance and slow to build. Asthmatic William, who found the polluted air of Whitehall Palace insufferable, was anxious to move to the country as soon as possible. A greater part of the Tudor palace would have to be reused. In consequence Hawksmoor made one of the most important and useful drawings for architectural historians: a survey of the Tudor palace recording what William and Mary were

to destroy (fig. 78). In the early summer of 1689, Henry VIII's lodgings and those of his queens still survived. Proposals were now made to replace these with new south and east fronts around a new eastern quadrangle, Fountain Court (fig. 83). Both King and Queen, as joint monarchs, would have equally grand State Apartments (fig. 79). Hawksmoor drew a scheme based partly on a design by Claude Perrault for Louis XIV's palace of the Louvre in Paris, with a giant pediment in the middle of the South Front and a dome at the centre of the east façade.

In plan, these designs were not dissimilar to the eventual scheme, but the third and final set of elevations showed a more restrained, box-like palace. As built, Hampton Court's East Front features a row of round windows and is topped by a balustrade (fig. 80). The architectural writer Roger North was unimpressed by the balustrade, saying it "looks like the teeth of a comb and doth in no sort answer the Grandeur of a Royall palace". A carved triangular pediment marks the position of the main room on the principal (first) floor, and masks a low attic

storey. Wren may have preferred to raise the *piano nobile* (containing the King's Apartments to the south and the Queen's to the east) slightly higher above the ground, but its level had to be carried through from the Great Hall and surviving first-floor lodgings of the Tudor palace.

Inside, the rooms were to be planned in a new manner. The gallery adjacent to William's rooms, the Cartoon Gallery, was unusually accessible for a royal long gallery: it opened directly into the Privy Chamber, the main room of parade in the middle of the South Front. The gallery was used for meetings of his council rather than as a private space for William himself. Like many features of the new Hampton Court, it was based directly on Versailles, the palace of William's arch-enemy Louis XIV, where a similar arrangement could be found. It was Mary, rather than her husband, who had the more detailed discussions with Wren, and she was left with the heavy responsibility of driving the works forward. During the building season William would frequently be away campaigning on the continent against the French forces.

### Building work begins, 1689–94

One of the first tasks undertaken on site in 1689 was the construction of two blocks of barracks for William's Foot and Horse Guards respectively (fig. 81), as protection for the vulnerable monarch. The barracks flanking the drive leading to the West Front were begun in May and completed by the end of the year; in 1700 they were linked up into one building by a 'sutlery' or provision room.

The building of the South Front of the new quadrangle began in June. The east range followed (fig. 82) and two years later the north range was begun as the lead roof on the east range was being completed. Hampton Court is well known for the glow of its red brick, but in fact Wren would have preferred to use more stone in the new work. His difficulty was that war against the French had made it dangerous for ships to carry stone up the Channel from Portland to London. In 1690, Mary complained that "want of money and of Portland Stone are the hindrances" to progress. Even work on Wren's new St Paul's Cathedral had ground to a halt for lack of supplies. Wren looked elsewhere: the carved swags on the South Front are made of Headington stone from Oxfordshire.

A builder's yard sprang up on the site of the Privy Garden to the south including a rubbing house for decorative brickwork, a forge for ironwork and a

RIGHT 83. *Fountain Court, William and Mary's new quadrangle. The row of round windows to the left is mirrored to the right by a row of panels painted by Louis Laguerre in 1691–94 with scenes from 'The Labours of Hercules'. William liked to associate himself with the hero Hercules, who performed nine superhuman labours. Caius Cibber's carving depicting 'Hercules triumphing over Envy' appears in the East Front's pediment (above).*

'closet' with a table for the architects' use. Many of the materials were not new: Tudor stone from the old palace was reused, boards were brought from Charles II's unfinished palace at Winchester and some of the joists in the Cartoon Gallery were simply Tudor timbers reshaped. The bricks themselves were bought from suppliers in Vauxhall and Twickenham; gravel was dug out of Hampton Court Green. Work forged ahead at a great pace until December, when disaster struck. A section of the spine wall running east and west through the centre of the south range collapsed and two carpenters died. Only weeks before, there had been a roof collapse at Wren's other project at Kensington Palace and a workman had been killed there too. The Queen blamed herself: she had been "too impatient" to complete her new houses and had demanded too much. "All this, as much as it was the fault of the workmen, humanly speaking", she wrote, "yet shewed

me plainly the hand of God was in it, and I was truly humbled."

Yet none of the workmen was willing to take the blame. On 13 January 1690, a hearing was held at the Treasury to determine the cause of the collapse, and to decide whether the rest of the building was safe. On one side stood Wren, supported by his Master Carpenter and his Master Mason. On the other stood Wren's architectural rival, the arrogant but successful William Talman; among his expert witnesses were a sculptor and a mason whose work Wren had previously criticized at St Paul's Cathedral. In this tense situation, Wren needed to convince the Lords of the Treasury that he had indeed intended to use structural ironwork in the South Front; Talman argued that it was a desperate afterthought to fix a bad design. Wren triumphed and was allowed to resume work. A further section of brickwork was taken down and rebuilt for safety. Talman, however, would soon have his revenge.

84. A blue-and-white japanned table, attributed to Daniel Marot, probably made for the Water Gallery at Hampton Court. This structure, to be demolished in the later phases of building the Baroque palace, was the principal original setting for Mary II's famed blue-and-white collection.

RIGHT 85. One of the blue-and-white cream pans from Mary's dairy in the Water Gallery, Delftware to designs by A. Koechs, c. 1694.

Meanwhile, Mary was using the Water Gallery as a small private house while work was in progress on the main palace. This Tudor brick structure, originally used for disembarking from royal barges, had last been used by Charles II's retired mistress Lady Castlemaine, latterly Duchess of Cleveland. She had constructed a dairy within the gallery, an aristocratic playroom like that of Louis XIV's mistress Louise de la Vallière at Versailles, rather than a functional office. Daniel Defoe described how Mary now created within the gallery "a set of lodgings, for her private retreat only, but most exquisitely furnished". He thought it "the pleasantest little Thing within Doors that could possibly be made". Mary had the gallery's casement windows converted into sashes and added extravagantly moulded plaster ceilings. A new boiler provided her with hot running water in a room large enough to have five sash windows, with paper shields over them for privacy. The dairy also had running water and was retiled in Delftware.

On the first floor was a gallery, hung with the paintings of "the principal ladies attending upon her majesty". These were the portraits in Sir Godfrey Kneller's series of the 'Hampton Court Beauties' that now hang in William III's Private Dining Room. The blue-and-white Delft tiles in the dairy provided the theme for the decoration throughout (fig. 85). Mary had become infected with the mania for interior decoration incorporating blue-and-white china while in The Netherlands, and at Het Loo William and Mary had employed the designer Daniel Marot to oversee the design of such china-based rooms for them (fig. 84). Mary's order books confirm that chairs for the Water Gallery were made in London, "painted in imitation of china for our service at Hampton Court". Daniel Marot was a member of the Queen's household, and he provided designs for the embroideries in the Queen's Closet that may well have been worked by Mary herself with the help of her ladies

(fig. 86). Despite the extravagance of the Water Gallery, it would shortly be pulled down and a new Privy Garden constructed over its site.

Mary, one of the most significant among all Hampton Court's royal patrons, spent only six years supervising work there. In December 1694, while at Kensington Palace, she discovered a rash on her arms. Recognizing it as a symptom of smallpox, then as now a fatal disease, she calmly set about ordering her unpaid bills and writing to her husband. "You can believe what a condition I am in, loving her as I do," he in turn wrote to a cousin. "If I should lose her, I shall have done with the world." On the 28th, Mary died. Despite its inauspicious beginning, theirs was a close marriage, and William was grief-stricken.

One consequence of Mary's death was that work stopped at Hampton Court. Her role as client had been vital, but a pause was necessary financially. The Queen and King had been spending at twice the rate of Charles II. They owed sixteen months' worth of salaries to their servants below stairs. A period of retrenchment was required, and nothing was done for three years.

## The completion of the King's State Apartments

In 1697 the Peace of Rijswijk was signed and William's war against the French came to an end. William found himself with time and money to spend at Hampton Court once again. He now had to solve the problem of how best to display the series of cartoons (designs for tapestries) by Raphael depicting the *Acts of the Apostles*. Made in 1516 for tapestries intended to be hung in the Sistine Chapel, they had been acquired by Charles I in 1623. Now the cartoons were glued together and put up in the specially modified Cartoon Gallery (fig. 88). Christopher Hatton reported that "the cartoons by Raphael ... were far beyond all the paintings I ever saw". (The cartoons on display now are copies, probably made

86. The Queen's Closet is hung with eight panels of embroidery, probably designed for Mary II by Daniel Marot. Although it was intended for her use, Mary died before this room could be completed.

BELOW 87. Detail of a Grinling Gibbons carving in the King's Withdrawing Room. The carver did not arrive in England until he was nineteen and always spoke with a Dutch accent. John Evelyn described him as "the greatest master both for invention and rareness of work that the world ever had in any age".

RIGHT 88. The Cartoon Gallery, hung with seventeenth-century copies of Raphael's famous cartoons. William and Mary had first ordered the cartoons to be unrolled in 1689 when they had just become King and Queen and were inspecting all their new possessions. The Duchess of Marlborough described Mary visiting Hampton Court and examining its contents in detail, even turning over the quilts on the beds in the way people did when visiting an inn.

by Henry Cooke in 1697, the originals having gone to the Victoria and Albert Museum in 1865.)

This was the first step in the process of finishing and furnishing the interiors. William called for an estimate from Wren for the completion of the State Apartments. But Wren's estimate (£6,800) was undercut by his old rival Talman's (£5,500), and Talman was duly commissioned to complete the Great Stair, Guard Chamber, Communication Gallery and "four rooms beyond to the King's Great Bedchamber". The elevations of the new Hampton Court had been informed by Wren's knowledge of the great French buildings of the day, such as the Louvre and Les Invalides; French taste was considered the height of fashion, then as always. The rooms inside owed an even greater debt to France. Charles II and James II had already introduced some of the habits and etiquette of the French court to England, and the trend continued. A suite of royal rooms, formerly known as a 'lodging', gradually became known by the French term of an 'apartment'.

Talman had to base his designs for the King's Apartments around the Tudor tapestries that were still to form the backbone of the rooms' decoration. Grinling Gibbons began work on the carving in 1699; he was to provide architectural mouldings and carved festoons over many of the doors. In the Privy Chamber, Eating Room and Withdrawing Room (fig. 87) he also made frames for the pictures over the mantelpieces and for downstairs in the King's Private Apartments. The furnishing of these apartments was left in the safe hands of Ralph, 1st Duke of Montagu, Master of the Great Wardrobe. He was an expert in fashion and style, having served as ambassador to France for five years. His London home, Montagu House, was a monument to French taste and had been decorated by French craftsmen.

The rooms at Hampton Court were to be relatively sparsely furnished, partly because of the smallness of the budget, but mainly because space had to be left for the crush of courtiers when the King was in residence. The windows of the outer rooms are so tall that their curtains have to be pulled up by strings into festoons that disappear into a carved box covered in white damask (fig. 90). In the more private rooms – the King's closets and gallery – there were red and

91. *The King's Private Dining Room, where Kneller's 'Hampton Court Beauties' are displayed. William III's dining table is set out with meringues and crystallized fruit for the third, or dessert, course of dinner.*

green curtains drawn sideways in the modern fashion. The decoration is carefully graded and becomes increasingly elaborate in the more private rooms further away from the King's Staircase. The staircase itself (fig. 89) was painted by the Italian – and, controversially, Catholic – artist Antonio Verrio, who also painted the ceilings of the two innermost rooms of the King's Apartments, the Great and Little Bedchambers. In the scheme for the staircase Verrio showed William III in triumphal mode, dominating a group of Roman emperors who represent the King's Catholic enemies, as well as a banquet of the gods denoting the peace and plenty William had brought. A prominent figure here as elsewhere in the decoration of the new work was William's classical hero, Hercules, with his distinctive club and lion-skin. The Guard Chamber at the top of the stairs would be constantly occupied. The weapons on the

walls were arranged by John Harris, the Furbisher of Small Arms at Hampton Court, but only the pikes, drums and armour survive from the seventeenth century. Most courtiers would pass through this room to reach the Presence Chamber and Privy Chamber with their canopied thrones, from there, according to status, to navigate deeper into the State Apartments.

As Hampton Court was completed for only a short period before William died, it is difficult to picture his daily life. However, he does seem to have appeared before his court more frequently at the evening gathering known as the 'drawing room' rather than dining in public in the Eating Room. He preferred to eat with his intimates, just come in from the hunt, in his Private Dining Room on the ground floor (fig. 91). Here, an alcove containing a marble sideboard and a basin of running water was used for serving wine and could be closed off from the dining room proper by a sliding panel. Under the almond-shaped eyes of Kneller's 'Beauties', which were moved here from the Water Gallery, William would frequently drink too much in his depressed and lonely later years.

Since the time of Charles II, the bedchamber had become the most important room in the palace for receiving visitors, rather than a private room for the king alone. It is likely that William received ambassadors in the Great Bedchamber, as Charles II had done before him. This room demonstrates William's devotion to French fashion, for his great red bed was probably a gift from Louis XIV to the diplomat the Earl of Jersey, William's Lord Chamberlain, who then presented it to the King. Louis XIV's own bedchamber, scene of his court's most significant ceremonies, had recently been enlarged and divided into two by a rail. William followed suit, bringing out from storage a rail made for Charles II and installing it around his bed in order to keep spectators back.

The Great Bedchamber was used for ceremony and the King would sleep elsewhere. While he also had a Little Bedchamber next door (fig. 92), he probably used his private apartments on the ground floor at night. Here a cosy panelled room was hung with paintings depicting night scenes. The King's Back Stairway linked the State Apartments on the upper floor to his private apartments below. This also provided access to the rooms of the King's favourite, Arnold Joost van Keppel, Earl of Albemarle, who occupied a suite on the ground floor.

## Grand opening

In 1699, the Lord Chamberlain's secretary Sir John Stanley had been given the task of allocating the lodgings at Hampton Court to the members of William III's household. Sir Christopher Wren had made a survey of the building and Stanley had merely to assign rooms to individuals. Those above the King's Apartments were reached by a narrow stair set within the thickness of the central spine of the building, so that their inhabitants would not disturb the royal occupants. Immediately below the Cartoon Gallery lay the small kitchens used among others by Mr Nice, the cook responsible for preparing William's newly fashionable drinking chocolate. Stanley's task was complicated by the King's interference, and in the end no one was pleased, finding his or her rooms too high, too small, or not grand enough.

Stanley's task was the final preparation for a long-awaited occasion. The palace, now transformed by the vision of William III and Mary II, was at last almost ready to receive the first full visit of the court. On 28 October, Robert Jennings reported that "the

92. *The ceiling of the King's Little Bedchamber by Antonio Verrio showing Mars asleep in the lap of Venus. The painted urns in the coving contain rose and orange trees, which symbolize the coming together of the royal houses of Stuart and Orange.*

93. Primula auricula *by Stephenus Cousijns. This plant came from the collection of Gaspar Fagel, Chief Pensionary of The Netherlands, and is depicted here in a flamboyant plant-pot. It is one of a series of paintings of Fagel's specimens commissioned by William III, who purchased the specimens themselves after Fagel's death. The plants, together with their attendant keeper Leonard Plukenet, were brought to Hampton Court to form part of Queen Mary's collection of exotics.*

94. *Design for the Great Fountain Garden by Daniel Marot, dated 1689. The thirteen fountains intended for this garden were constructed but never put into working order. Ornate iron gates by Jean Tijou separated the garden from the park. Beyond the gates lie the two secondary avenues added by William and Mary to Charles II's central Long Water Avenue. The one to the left lines up on Kingston church, while the right-hand avenue leads to Thames Ditton.*

King's apartment is finished, and I fancy 'twill be made the prettiest place in the world. The king will give us all country apartments; we shall be much there, for he likes the place extremely." Although the courtiers' lodgings were still hurriedly being decorated, this was the end of the lengthy process of designing and building. In the meantime, William had lost his popularity, he was a sorrowing widower

and the opportunity for the devoted couple to enjoy their ambitious building project together had never materialized.

As William had decided to use the Cartoon Gallery for meetings of his council, he found himself without a private gallery for exercise or informal conversation. He commandeered the first-floor Queen's Gallery, which had been planned for his wife on the East Front. This room was now decorated in green mohair, with back-chairs covered in matching green. In 1702 the walls were hung with Mantegna's paintings of the *Triumphs of Caesar*, which had been restored first by Parry Walton and secondly by Louis Laguerre. The rest of the Queen's Apartments stood unfinished and empty.

## The transformation of the gardens

Meanwhile, as the courtiers settled into their new apartments, work was under way on the gardens outside. The Hampton Court gardens were the culmination of William's many years' experience of creating gardens in The Netherlands. Mary's collection of exotic plants from around the world was famous (fig. 93); she employed a botanical curator for them, Dr Leonard Plukenet, at a salary of £200 a year. The details of the largest parterre ever created in the seventeenth century were under discussion even before the East Front of the palace was completed. The Great Fountain Garden was to contain thirteen fountains powered by the Longford River, occupying the semicircle of land between the palace and the park. Daniel Marot was paid just over £236 for its design in 1689 (fig. 94). Some areas were *parterre de broderie* (box hedges and gravel) while others were *gazon coupé* (grass and gravel

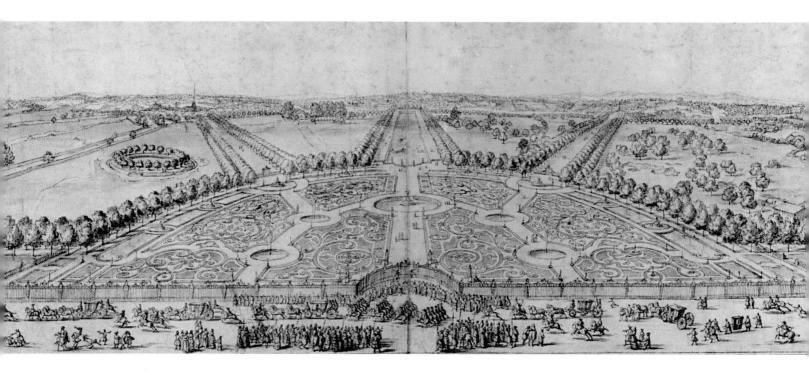

96. During its construction the Banqueting House, seen here from the roof of the palace, was known as 'The New Building in the Glass Case Garden', the glass cases being used for the cultivation of tender plants. The adjacent Pond Gardens contain Tudor walls and the remains of the Tudor fishponds that were later made into gardens by Queen Mary II. The ponds, used for breeding fish for the table, were fed by water overflowing from the fountain in Clock Court.

intermingled in a complex design best appreciated from above).

On the South Front, garden works had to wait until the 1690s after the builders' yard had been cleared away. The King's Private Apartments on the ground-floor level incorporated an Orangery (the Upper Orangery) complete with stoves and orange trees, and its doors could be opened wide to allow the interior to flow into the exterior. The Tudor mount was removed in 1690 and it took ten years for the final form of William's Privy Garden to appear. Not until William's partial recovery from Mary's death, "that sorrow being dispelled", did he carry out a plan to extend his garden right down to the river. Although Talman submitted an estimate for the work, this time it was the gardener Henry Wise who was successful. However, Wise's project was marked by a major intervention on William's part. In June 1701, the Privy Garden was nearing completion, with its new fountain, terraces and boundary walls in place. The wrought-iron screens by Jean Tijou (fig. 95) were slung between poles to demonstrate the effect of their intended position between the garden and the river. However, viewing the arrangements from his first-floor State Apartments, William was dissatisfied because he could not see the water. He decided to lower the southern end of the garden by 3 feet (90 cm). This meant that plants and water pipes had to be removed and replaced at an expense of over £1000. This was but a tiny part of the final total, which must

have been in the region of £155,000. Five statues, *Bacchus, Ceres, Apollo and Marsyas, Vulcan* and *Apollo,* stood in each of the compartments. Further embellishments included sundials, lead urns, a central fountain, stone steps and, to the west, the long elm-wood bower running along the top of a bank (fig. 97).

To the west of the Privy Garden lay the garden containing the Tudor ponds, now vastly improved with the construction of a Glass Case Garden and a new

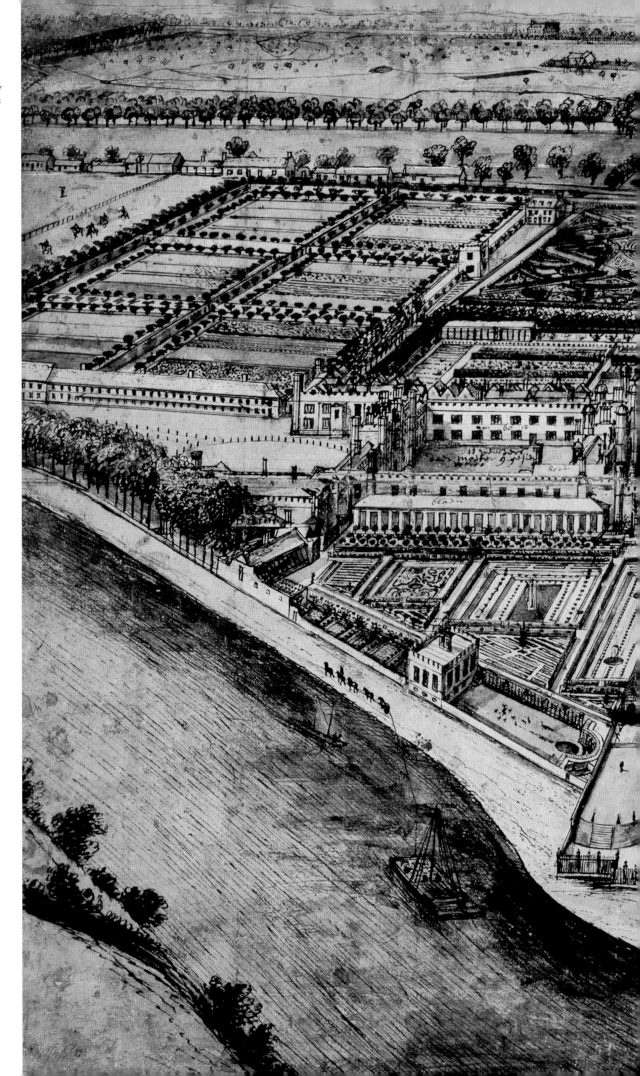

97. The Netherlandish artist Leonard Knyff is famous for his bird's-eye views of English country estates. Many were later engraved and published by John Kip. Knyff wrote to a client on 9 January 1703, "I have done a great many [drawings] of Hampton Courte and Windsor for his Highness [Prince George of Denmark] which are not yet engraved, I not being payd for them." This view shows the palace from the south in c. 1702, when William III's Privy Garden had replaced that of Henry VIII and other monarchs.

98. *The main room in the Banqueting House overlooks the river and was intended for small-scale entertainment. It is decorated with murals depicting, on the ceiling, Minerva as the Goddess of Wisdom, surrounded by the arts and sciences and, on the walls, the loves of Jupiter. The paintings probably combine the work of Antonio Verrio and his assistants.*

76

Banqueting House (fig. 96). The former contained three greenhouses built to Dutch designs for Mary's exotic plants. William replaced them with the single surviving second Orangery (the Lower Orangery) after her death. To the south, across the ponds, the Banqueting House has been described as "Talman's most important and original surviving work at Hampton Court". The brick exterior with its battlemented roof blends in with the Tudor surroundings, but it contains a dramatic painted interior by Verrio and others, quite sumptuously up to date (fig. 98). The Banqueting House was the first stage of a plan to create a *menagerie* like Louis XIV's at Versailles, though at Hampton Court work only got as far as the

aviary in its garden, containing oak birdcages and eighteen nesting boxes with bird-sized ramps leading up to them.

A further improvement to the gardens took place to the north, where William laid out the Wilderness Garden (fig. 99) in what had once been the Tudor orchard. The Wilderness was a fairly formal style of garden by modern standards. It consisted of a number of interconnected paths bordered by neatly clipped high hedges of hornbeam, creating a geometrical network of pathways in which the wanderer could pleasurably lose his or her way.

One of the compartments of the Wilderness took this concept to its extreme: it was laid out with the

*99. The earliest representation of the Maze at Hampton Court is to be found on this anonymous plan of the palace and its gardens, executed in the Office of Works, c. 1714. The surviving Maze is in the bottom left compartment of the (northern) Wilderness Garden. Other spirals and labyrinths shown are no longer in existence.*

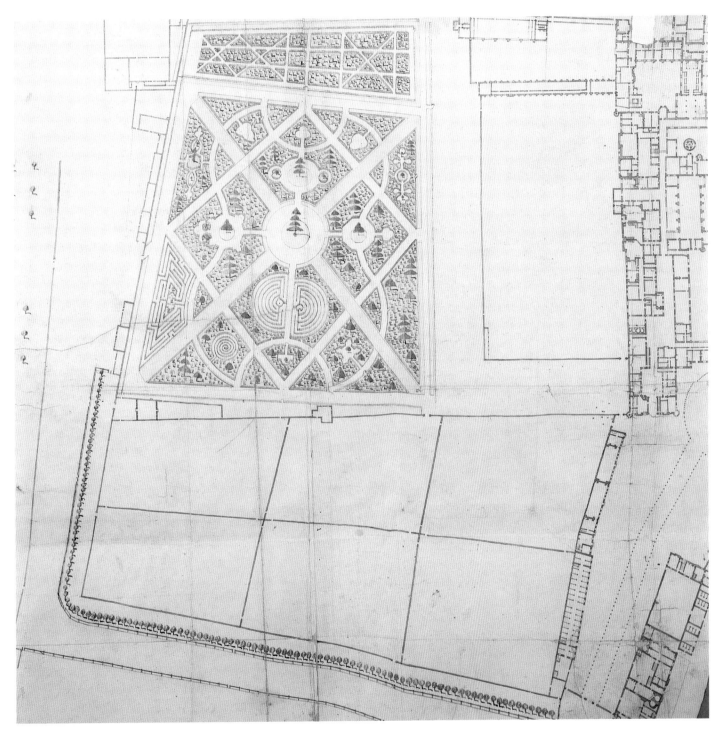

100. *The Maze is the only surviving compartment of the once extensive Wilderness that lay to the north of the palace. It was originally planted in deciduous hornbeam. The tough yew of the hedges today comes from a twentieth-century replanting, as the original hornbeam hedges were damaged by the huge number of visitors who flocked here in the nineteenth and twentieth centuries.*

101. *J. Tinney after Anthony Highmore,* The Pavilions belonging to the Bowling Green, at the End of the Terras Walk, at Hampton Court, *c. 1744. The four pavilions around the oval-shaped bowling green were designed by William Talman as retiring places for William III and his courtiers between games. One, the 'king's pavilion', contained mirror frames and cornices carved by Grinling Gibbons.*

tight twists and turns of Hampton Court's famous Maze (fig. 100). William III had previously created a maze at his Dutch home of *Huis ten Bosch,* the 'House in the Wood'. Because the documentary evidence is sparse, historians continue to debate exactly when the Hampton Court Maze was planted. Notwithstanding its slightly mysterious origins, William III's courtiers probably found the paths between its hedges as amusing and enticing as visitors do today. In 1724 Daniel Defoe would describe the "labyrinth" as "not only well designed, and completely finished, but ... perfectly well kept". Originally the Wilderness contained four mazes, all but one of which are now lost.

Still this is not the end of the list of pleasant places made for William III. A short walk away along the river to the east, he had the Bowling Green and its four pavilions reconstructed to Talman's designs (fig. 101). Each pavilion, similar to those used for Louis XIV when off duty at his country palace at

Marly, contained three rooms on its upper floor. One pavilion survives, though much altered, as a private house in the park.

## The King's death

On 20 February 1702, when William was riding his horse Sorrel out from Hampton Court, the animal stumbled and he fell, breaking his collarbone. He had the bone set, then misguidedly travelled to Kensington Palace. Here, after a few days of deteriorating health, he died.

Why had Sorrel tripped? Rumours soon began to circulate. The Jacobites, supporters of the claims of the Catholic sons of the deposed James II against the Protestant King William, drank toasts to a certain "little gentleman in black velvet": the Hampton Court mole whose hill had caused the death of the King. But the new palace was built and the Protestant kingdom was secure, twin legacies of William and Mary.

# *Two* QUEENS and *Two* GEORGES 1702–60

## ANNE, GEORGE I, GEORGE II and CAROLINE

The Baroque palace comes into full use in the reign of Queen Anne, last of the Stuart monarchs. Under George I and George II the palace is completed but the court – perennially split by father–son rivalry – ceases to visit after Queen Caroline's death in 1737.

102. *The Queen's State Bedchamber, left incomplete after the death of Mary II for whom it was intended and finished for the Prince and Princess of Wales only in 1717. The room still retains its original crimson silk damask bed, made for the royal couple in 1715.*

### Queen Anne (1702–1714)

When Queen Anne (fig. 103) came to the throne in succession to her brother-in-law, William III, the era of grand spending on Hampton Court Palace was brought to a swift close. Significant work continued, both within the palace and in the gardens and estate, but the main shape that survives to this day (see fig. 1) had already been laid down.

Anne was constantly beset by money worries. She was reluctant to settle William's outstanding debts on the palace and many craftsmen went unpaid. The grant made by Parliament was insufficient for her needs, especially when the revenues on which it was based failed to yield the expected returns. The Office of Works was, if anything, in even worse financial straits. Anne was committed to expensive military ventures, at least until Marlborough's magnificent victory over Louis XIV and France at Blenheim in 1704. The Queen also had constant health worries. In her younger years she was almost continually pregnant, but of seventeen pregnancies only one son survived even into childhood. In later years, especially after she was widowed, she grew obese and suffered from gout along with a host of other ailments.

Added to these difficulties was the politically and socially inconvenient fact that the reigning monarch was a woman. Although Anne occupied the apartments designed for the king's use at each of her palaces, the advantage of ready access to a male monarch by male courtiers was now lost. Anne

103. *Queen Anne by Sir Godfrey Kneller. By the end of her life the Queen had become so obese and diseased that she was barely able to walk. In 1704 Morden published a short poem in praise of Anne at Hampton Court:*

*Here our blest Queen's
    magnificence yet reigns,
O'er death's proud empire
    and its mournful trains.
Here Italy and Spain are
    clearly seen,
In richest fruits, trees, shades,
    in walks and greens.*

herself was painfully shy and lacked the political acumen of William. Even her close companion Sarah, Duchess of Marlborough, the wife of the Blenheim victor and Groom of the Stole, said the Queen retained in her prodigious memory "very little besides ceremonies and customs of courts and suchlike insignificant trifles". The reign of Queen Anne was a watershed, ushering in an age of party politics and cabinet government in which the monarch became

William, Duke of Gloucester, the only one of Queen Anne's children to survive beyond infancy, was born at Hampton Court on 24 July 1689 and christened in the Chapel Royal.

When Alexander Pope visited the palace in 1717 he recorded his impressions of the dreariness of court life: "I heard of no ball, assembly, basset table or any place, where two or three were gathered together."

Among Queen Caroline's Ladies of the Bedchamber was her husband's mistress, Henrietta Howard. The Queen took delight in seeing that Mrs Howard was given the most menial tasks to perform.

more of a ceremonial figure, less a focus of political activity and patronage.

Although Hampton Court Palace had barely been finished it now became a secondary royal residence. The Queen preferred Windsor as a country retreat, just as in London her preference was for Kensington Palace rather than the sovereign's official seat, St James's Palace. Hampton Court was mainly a place for business, being midway between central London and Windsor and so quite convenient for politicians to assemble there for Privy Council meetings. In the first six years of her reign, Anne spent only three nights in the palace. Her beloved husband Prince George of Denmark – "very fat, loves news, his bottle and the Queen", as one contemporary described him – died in 1708. After this Anne made greater use of Hampton Court, and in the last four years of her life devoted her efforts to improving and embellishing it.

When William III died, the principal building works at Hampton Court were complete. The East Front contained the shell of the range intended as the Queen's Apartments, unfinished since Mary II's death in 1694. The intertwined monogram of William and Mary poignantly forms one of the principal decorative motifs on the exterior of the range. One of Anne's early artistic commissions was to Antonio Verrio. Once he had completed the painted decoration on the magnificent King's Staircase, he was given the task of providing the decorative scheme for the Queen's Drawing Room. The principal room in the East Front, it was centred on the Long Water Canal and the formal gardens. This room was almost certainly fitted out for Prince George, who features twice in its decoration. On the north wall of the room he stands dressed as Lord High Admiral, reviewing the fleet; on the opposite wall he appears naked and plump, lying on the back

of a sea creature with cherubs disporting themselves around him (fig. 104). The rest of the decorative scheme glorifies Anne and British naval power. Around this magnificence, other rooms remained unfinished; some even still had no floorboards.

In 1707 the Astronomical Clock and the cupola above Anne Boleyn's Gateway were both overhauled, and a new mechanism was provided for the clock. These were among the few exterior works undertaken at Hampton Court in the first half of Anne's reign. Other works followed when Anne stayed at the palace more often. She resided there for a total of five months in 1710, 1711 and 1713. Various alterations were made to the disposition of the King's Apartments, reflecting both the Queen's position as a female monarch for whom the ceremonial *levée* was somewhat inappropriate and her general ill-health. The back stairs were used much more frequently as a means of access to her by courtiers, ambassadors and petitioners, and the private State Rooms were remodelled to reflect that.

When the court was in residence the palace was full and busy once more, a centre of political intrigue and decision-making. Alexander Pope described in his poem *The Rape of the Lock* (1712) the assemblies, jockeying for preferment and social ritual of the reinvigorated Hampton Court:

> Here Thou, Great Anna!
> Whom three Realms obey,
> Dost sometimes Counsel take –
> and sometimes Tea.

The greatest impact that Queen Anne had upon the fabric of the palace was in the remodelling of the Chapel Royal (fig. 106). As a firm upholder of the Anglican faith and royal tradition, she maintained a

full complement of chapel musicians. As a sick woman who did not care for the elaborate etiquette of the Bedchamber, she saw her daily attendance at Chapel as her main opportunity to make a public appearance. In 1710 Wren and Hawksmoor successfully presented schemes for remodelling the body of the Chapel; these included a grand timber reredos at the east end with a painted scene by James Thornhill above, the removal of the Tudor window tracery and the addition of panelling, box pews, an organ and new sanctuary fittings. A staircase was added leading down from the Royal Pew, where Thornhill also painted the central ceiling with a playful scene of cherubs in the heavens holding aloft a crown and a sword (fig. 105). The work was completed in 1712.

When she was at Hampton Court but not in her bed or her pew, the Queen could be found in the park indulging her love of hunting. Unable to ride on horseback, she followed the hunt in a two-wheeled chaise for which twenty miles (32 km) of new rides were cut through Home Park and Bushy Park. Whether the Queen was quite as skilled as Jonathan Swift described her in 1711 has been open to question: "The queen was abroad today in order to hunt, but finding it disposed to rain she kept in her coach; she hunts in a chaise with one horse, which she drives herself, and drives furiously like Jehu, and is a mighty hunter like Nimrod." Certainly she was vigorous, as on another occasion Swift recorded that "The queen was hunting the stag till four this afternoon, and she drove in her chaise above forty miles, and it was five before we went to dinner."

In contrast to the limited work inside the palace, the gardens were on the whole well maintained. There was a complete remodelling of the Great Parterre and the Great Fountain Garden, which included dismantling many of the fountains and providing new ornamental stretches of water. Henry Wise, who became the royal gardener in 1702, supervised the scheme (fig. 107). He simplified the layout,

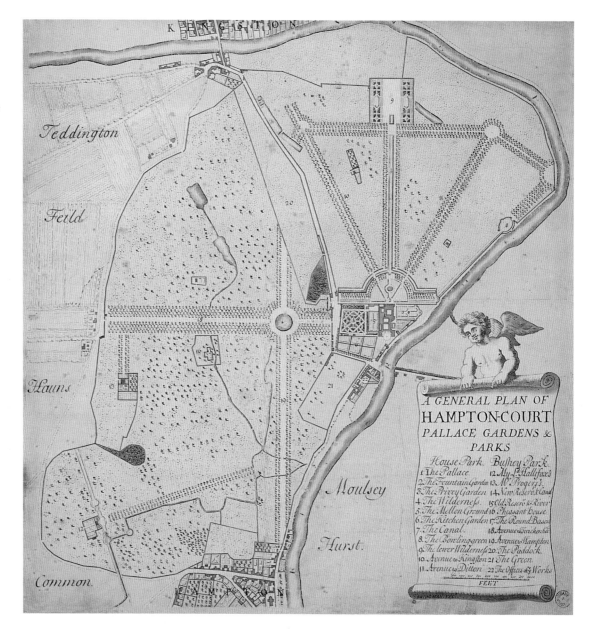

107. Charles Bridgeman, A General Plan of Hampton Court Palace Gardens and Parks, 1711. This important survey of the Hampton Court estate at the end of Queen Anne's reign records the alterations made to the gardens by Henry Wise. From 1726 Bridgeman worked in partnership with Wise and succeeded him as Master Gardener in 1728, a post he held until his death in 1738.

removed the box hedging (the smell of which, according to Daniel Defoe, Queen Anne detested) and the cut turf patterns, but kept the yew trees. The result was a simpler garden design in grass and gravel that was more English in taste than the French inspiration of the preceding reign (fig. 111). The ironwork screen by Jean Tijou was finally put in its intended place at the river end of the Privy Garden. The Lion Gate, a grand new north entrance to the gardens from Bushy Park, was planned although it was not completed until the following reign. With its military motifs this was almost certainly the work of Sir John Vanbrugh, playwright and gentleman-architect, who was to come to greater prominence at the palace after the Queen's death.

## George I and the Hanoverian dynasty (1714–1727)

Anne died in August 1714. The following month her successor arrived to claim his new kingdom: George, Elector of Hanover. A stout Protestant (in both senses), the great-grandson of James I through the female line (his grandmother had been Elizabeth, the Winter Queen of Bohemia), he came to the throne as George I (fig. 110). The King brought German courtiers and Turkish servants, his mistresses (he had divorced his wife in 1694 and locked her away), and his son, the future George II, with his wife Caroline of Ansbach (figs. 108, 109) and their young family. The new King also supported the Whigs politically, in contrast to the favour the old

ABOVE 110. *Portrait miniature of George I in his coronation robes by Bernard Lens, c. 1714. The King's accession was swiftly followed by the failed attempt of the 'Old Pretender', James Edward Stuart, heir to James II, to regain the throne, and the strength of the Hanoverian dynasty was confirmed.*

BELOW LEFT 108. *Sir James Thornhill's portrait of George, Prince of Wales in the coving of the Queen's State Bedchamber. As George II, with Queen Caroline at his side, he oversaw the final flowering of court life at the palace. The Lord Chamberlain had wanted to give the commission for this ceiling painting to Sebastiano Ricci but the Earl of Halifax, First Lord of the Treasury, supported Thornhill as a fellow countryman and declared that "if Ricci painted it, he would not pay him". Thornhill was given the work and received £457 10s. The Board of Works considered the ceiling "skilfully and laboriously performed".*

BELOW RIGHT 109. *Sir James Thornhill's matching portrait of Caroline, Princess of Wales in the coving of the Queen's State Bedchamber. King George I and Frederick, later Prince of Wales, are also portrayed on the ceiling.*

queen had bestowed on their Tory rivals. Many Tories were implicated in the 1715 Jacobite rebellion, which was intended to return the exiled Stuart line, in the shape of Queen Anne's Catholic half-brother James, to the throne. With the abject failure of the rising, they were to be consigned to the political wilderness for a generation.

George I also smiled upon Hampton Court Palace, where Vanbrugh was his preferred designer, assisted at first by Nicholas Hawksmoor. Sir Christopher Wren, who had dominated the royal building programme and the Office of Works for so long, was ousted in 1718 and a new generation of architects took control. The main work at the palace was to fit out suitably impressive suites of rooms for the Prince and Princess of Wales on the queen's side of the palace: the Bedchamber, Drawing Room and Privy Chamber. Lord Hervey, whose journals provide vivid descriptions of court life in the subsequent reign, wrote that "the pageantry and splendour, the badges and trappings of royalty, were as pleasing to the son as they were irksome to the father".

### Father and son

The abiding theme of the Hanoverian era was the loathing between royal fathers and their eldest sons, who in turn hated their own eldest sons. The often bitter enmity between George I and George II, George II and Prince Frederick, Frederick and George III, and finally George III and George IV was in itself the focus of political intrigue. In George I's

reign Hampton Court became the country version of Leicester House, the London home of the Prince of Wales, which attracted both a political opposition and an alternative artistic group. The first of many occasions when father and son showed their distinctly different approaches came in 1716 when George I returned to Hanover, leaving the Prince of Wales in charge (but stopping short of making him Regent). The Prince led a glittering court and conducted political business at Hampton Court Palace throughout those summer months.

Of the rooms that were newly fitted out for the Prince and Princess in 1716, the most significant was the State Bedchamber, sumptuously furnished with a new state bed under a ceiling by Thornhill, the walls hung with Stuart royal portraits (fig. 102). The decorative scheme proclaimed the rightful descent of the crown to the Hanoverian princes. In addition to the State Rooms, the royal couple were provided with a number of private rooms in the north-east corner of the State Apartments, including a bathroom and dressing-room each. A range of new furniture including gilded mirrors, pier tables and stands was supplied by the cabinet-makers John Gumley and James Moore. Their private bedroom still retains the night lock system by which the Prince or Princess could lie in bed and control the doors by a system of wires and bolts.

In 1716, and then again in 1717 when the King resided at Hampton Court together with his son and daughter-in-law, these rooms must have been

111. *The Great Fountain Garden looking east. Queen Anne was keen to reduce expenditure on the royal gardens and the Great Fountain Garden was much simplified during her reign. In 1703 Henry Wise submitted an estimate for "sinking, new making and altering" the garden, which was done that same year. William and Mary's thirteen marble fountains were reduced in number to five and the parterre de broderie was swept away. In 1707 the garden was remodelled again: eighty-eight topiary hollies and yews were removed and the garden was returfed and gravelled. Stephen Switzer described their new appearance as "plain but noble".*

TOP LEFT 112. *Queen Caroline's Bathroom, fitted out for her as Princess of Wales. The room and its furnishings were restored in 1995. The Queen would have sat on a stool inside the tub while she bathed. The marble cistern provided cold water; hot water was brought in from the back stairs by the Queen's Necessary Woman.*

ABOVE 113. *R. Reeve after R. Cattermole,* Banqueting Hall (the Queen's Guard Chamber). *From W.H. Pyne's* Royal Residences *(1817–20). The illustration shows the Guard Chamber after its occupation by the refugee William V of Orange before 1802. When first completed for the Prince and Princess of Wales the room was painted white and glazed to give the effect of stone. It was furnished with beds, benches and a table for the Yeomen of the Guard.*

TOP RIGHT 114. *Detail of the fireplace in the Queen's Guard Chamber, embodying the wit of Sir John Vanbrugh and the skill of Grinling Gibbons. Gibbons was discovered by John Evelyn and presented to Charles II in 1671. His early work was rejected by the King but he was later granted royal patronage and was employed at Windsor, Whitehall and Kensington, as well as at Hampton Court. He was made Master Carver to the Crown in 1693.*

swarming with builders and decorators as soon and as often as there was opportunity. The works programme was extended in 1717 to include the decoration of the Guard Chamber (fig. 113) and Presence Chamber, the two rooms that completed the formal circuit of the State Apartments, fulfilling the vision of William and Mary. These rooms were designed by Sir John Vanbrugh. The scheme included the over-sized figures of Yeomen of the Guard that flank the Guard Chamber fireplace (fig. 114), which have been attributed to Grinling Gibbons, and the two massive, idiosyncratic fireplaces in other rooms. The Prince's suite even acquired a new kitchen – the austere block to the north of the palace, known today as the Georgian House (fig. 115) – which some now claim to be by Colen Campbell and the first eighteenth-century Neo-Palladian English building.

The summer of 1717 at Hampton Court proved to be not the reconciliation between father and son that many had hoped for, but instead the opening skirmishes of a family war that would last another ten years. After 1717 the Queen's Private Apartments were used no more (until George and Caroline had themselves become King and Queen in 1727), as the Prince of Wales had set up his own rival summer court at Richmond Lodge.

### George I stamps his mark

The King was now determined to make an even bigger splash at Hampton Court. In 1718 the Tudor Tennis Court was refurbished, hung with sailcloth

LEFT 115. *The Georgian House, built as a separate kitchen block in 1717 for George I to designs possibly by Colen Campbell. This new building provided food for the King's table and was known as the 'German' kitchen, as it was staffed by the cooks and servants that he had brought to England in 1715. The old Tudor kitchen range was used to feed the household and became known as the 'English' kitchen, as it was staffed with English servants. In the 1780s the Georgian House was converted into dwellings and later became the residence of the Superintendent of the Palace; today the eastern half is available for holiday lets through the Landmark Trust.*

BELOW LEFT 116. *Thomas Fort's survey of the Great Hall set up as a theatre, c. 1718. Only with the antiquarian revival almost a century later was Henry VIII's hall uncovered once more. The stage may be seen at the top; the canvas scenery was painted by Thornhill. Thomas Fort was Clerk of Works at the palace from 1714 until his death in 1745. This is one of an album of some forty drawings of the palace attributed to him.*

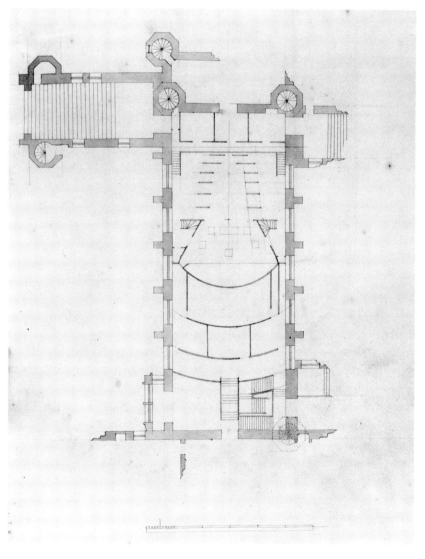

and converted for use as a grand assembly room, while the Great Hall was converted into a theatre (fulfilling the intentions of William III, who had begun to fit it out for the purpose) (fig. 116). This work was probably undertaken by Vanbrugh, who was himself a playwright and theatre impresario. Curtains covered the large windows, boxes and seats were installed, and the assembled audience faced west towards the stage erected in front of the screens passage. Sir Richard Steele's company from Drury Lane performed seven plays before the assembled court, including *Hamlet* and *Henry VIII* by Shakespeare, both appropriate to the setting.

The court of George I had been relatively informal compared with that of preceding kings. The polished etiquette of the Bedchamber and the *levée* hardly outlived William III. The King occupied the full set of rooms built for William, removing some of the partitions that had formed suites on the ground floor of the South Front for William's favourites. George I dined formally but usually not in state, so lesser mortals could join him at his table, and he preferred to preside over assemblies. He also instituted a more rigid separation between his private and his public apartments. The Gentlemen of the Bedchamber organized admission to the royal presence, guiding visitors up the back stairs to a closet accessible from the King's bedroom, where they were received.

In the years following the 1718 visit, ambitious plans for the wholesale remodelling of Hampton Court were drawn up by Vanbrugh, but came to nothing. The Queen's Apartments were completed

with the addition of an octagonal private oratory. Its rich and distinctive late-seventeenth-century domed plaster ceiling had been kept in store for some thirty years and was installed in 1719. The King paid occasional visits to the palace, usually to hunt, but otherwise it sat shut up and idle, waiting for its next blaze of glory under the new monarch.

## George II and Queen Caroline (1727–1760)

When George II succeeded his father in 1727, Hampton Court Palace entered its final phase as a principal royal residence. King George and Queen Caroline were more frequent visitors than their

immediate predecessors, especially the Queen, who regularly spent summers at Hampton Court when the King was away in Hanover. The work begun ten years before on the private rooms in the Queen's Apartments was completed.

The following seasons at the royal court are among the most colourfully documented of any, through the memoirs and letters of Lord John Hervey, who was made Vice-Chamberlain in the round of political appointments by the prime minister, Sir Robert Walpole, in April 1730. Hervey became the particular confidant of Queen Caroline, although he had first become an intimate of Frederick, Prince of Wales who – true to Hanoverian form – warred continuously with his parents.

### Court life

As Vice-Chamberlain, Hervey's main duty was the daily organization and upkeep of the royal palaces. This included assigning courtiers' lodgings within the palaces, supervising the arrangements for moving the court physically from one palace to another, and planning special events. In any absence of the Chamberlain, the Duke of Grafton, Hervey also had to officiate at important state occasions. With his own lodgings usually located at the foot of the Queen's back stairs, Hervey was in a strategic position to control private access to the royal presence and to know courtiers' movements.

Soon after he arrived at court, Hervey wrote to his lover Stephen Fox with a description of how he spent his time:

We jog on here *le vieux train* [in our usual way]. A little walking, a little hunting and a little playing; a little flattering, a little railing and a little lying; a little hate, a little friendship, and a little love; a little hope and a little fear, a little joy and a little pain.

Days usually started slowly, then courtiers went walking, hunting or riding unless there was a formal drawing-room assembly. Every afternoon, before or after the 3 pm dinner (depending on the season), ladies walked in the gardens or parks, gossiping and flirting with their admirers (fig. 118). The evenings were given to board or card games as well as dancing. "No mill-horse ever went in a more constant track, or more unchanging circle", as Hervey put it. Tea was one of the lubricants of fashionable daytime activity, which distressed Hervey's father, the Earl of Bristol, who wrote to his son, "I can feel little or no abatement of my pain till I have heard that you are finally determined to drink no more of that detestable, fatal liquor."

Although there was a prescribed daily and weekly pattern, life at Hampton Court, a summer residence, was less formal in its routine than the winter season at St James's Palace. The winter always saw a round of receptions and high protocol, although there was generally a higher level of formality at all the palaces than had been the case at George I's court. When they dined in public, the King and Queen usually had a crowd of onlookers – their table at Hampton Court was described in 1733 as "surrounded by benches to the very ceiling, which are filled with an infinite number of spectators". There were days for the conduct of formal business, including the King's morning *levée* when he received ministers, ambassadors and other guests, and a formal 'drawing room' in the later evening in which the royal family would circulate before retiring to the private apartments, where closer friends could attend on them.

When the court resided there the palace was full to bursting. All the members of the royal family had their own bodies of servants. Every officer of the royal household had the right to occupy an apartment. Others found accommodation where they could, within the palace or close at hand. Significant improvements were made in 1731, with new furnishings for all the courtiers' lodgings. If the royal household incurred expense, that paled into insignificance against the outlay of individual courtiers on dress, jewels, trinkets and living. For the many hundreds who attended at court, it was – as it had been for centuries – an expensive place to be but it held out the hope of preferment to office or an advantageous marriage. In the poem *On a Certain Lady at Court*, written in or around 1725, Alexander Pope satirized the dissembling, spite-driven gossip and

119. *John Spyers,* Outer Green Court, *c. 1780, showing the now demolished Houses of Offices (left) and the surviving Barrack Block (right) to the west of the palace. Spyers worked as a draughtsman for the royal gardener Lancelot 'Capability' Brown from 1764 to 1783. Two albums of his drawings of Hampton Court were purchased by Catherine the Great in the early 1780s for 1000 roubles and have recently come to light in The Hermitage, St Petersburg.

120. *George II's Gateway, Clock Court. William Kent replaced the Tudor royal range with an early essay in Georgian gothic; the four Maiano roundels were reset in the gateway. The principal rooms provided the suite for the Duke of Cumberland. The King's initials and the date 1732 over the gateway record the building of the new range.*

BELOW 121. *Attributed to Thomas Fort, the east elevation of Clock Court, 1727. This is a rare detailed view, prior to their replacement by William Kent in 1732, of the decayed royal lodgings built by Cardinal Wolsey for Henry VIII, Catherine of Aragon and Princess Mary.*

flirtation, the fawning on the most powerful courtiers for the advantages they could confer, that formed the stuff of court life:

> I know the thing that's most uncommon
> (Envy be silent and attend!);
> I know a reasonable woman,
> Handsome and witty, yet a friend.
>
> Not warped by passion, awed by rumour,
> Not grave through pride or gay through folly;
> An equal mixture of good humour
> And sensible soft melancholy.
>
> "Has she no faults, then (Envy says), sir?"
> Yes, she has one, I must aver:
> When all the world conspires to praise her,
> The woman's deaf, and does not hear.

Such arch criticism rankled. In his anonymous "Epistle to a Doctor of Divinity from a Nobleman at Hampton Court", written in 1733, Lord Hervey directed his satire back against Pope:

> ... Like you, we lounge & feast & play & chatter
> In private satirize, in public flatter.

Such was the cut and thrust of court life. By the time these lines were written, political opposition revolved around the figure of Prince Frederick and his court. Relations between father and son continued at a low ebb, and Hervey noted how the King barely acknowledged the presence of the Prince of Wales: "Whenever the Prince was in a room with the King, it put one in mind of stories one has heard of ghosts that appear to be part of the company and are invisible to the rest." Sir Robert Walpole thought that Frederick was a "poor, weak, irresolute, false, lying, dishonest, contemptible wretch that nobody loves, that nobody believes, that nobody will trust". The Prince's own mother, Queen Caroline, was no kinder, saying she could not stand the sight of the "avaricious, sordid monster" who was "the greatest beast in the whole world".

Despite the growing animosity between father and son, some of the most distinctive contributions to the ensemble at Hampton Court Palace were the newly refurbished rooms for the Prince of Wales in the north-east corner of the State Apartments. These were elaborately redecorated and refurnished in green and silver in 1728. Throughout the palace there was a programme of refurbishment and modernization that continued for the ten years following George II's accession, creating a suitable setting for the court on its regular summer forays. In 1731 the King refurbished the State Apartments and extended his private apartments, for both of which most of the new furnishings and fittings were supplied by Benjamin Goodison. Meanwhile, the Queen's Gallery was hung with the recently acquired Alexander tapestries. Verrio's murals in the Queen's Drawing Room, disliked by Queen Caroline, were covered with green damask and the nine Mantegna paintings of the *Triumphs of Caesar* purchased by Charles I were hung on top.

This programme of work was swiftly followed by the scheme for the Cumberland Suite, fitted out for the King's younger son William, Duke of Cumberland. For the favoured son, little expense was spared in making a suitable set of apartments in the range running between Fountain Court and Clock Court. This was a survivor from Wolsey's Tudor palace, incorporating the rooms Henry VIII had originally designated for his first queen, but it was in a parlous condition (fig. 121). The new range was designed by William Kent in a self-consciously gothic style, wrapped around the Tudor core that remains at the heart of the new building (fig. 120). The Tudor,

122. *Philippe Mercier,* The Music Party: Frederick, Prince of Wales with his Three Eldest Sisters, *painted in 1733 when Prince Frederick began playing the cello. Lord Hervey reported that by 1734 it was the Prince's practice when at Kensington to "sing French and Italian songs to his own playing, for an hour or two together, while his audience was composed of all the under servants and rabble of the Palace". There is another version of this picture with the sitters in front of the Dutch House, now known as Kew Palace.*

gothic and Jacobean elements in Kent's design, both inside and outside the range, were a deliberate attempt to make a fitting complement to the original sixteenth-century fabric, in contrast to the bravura colonnade designed by Wren on the south side of Clock Court as the approach to the King's Apartments.

The final embellishment of the palace under George II was the completion of the Queen's Staircase, again by William Kent (who had previously been favoured by George I with the commission for the decorative schemes in the State Apartments at Kensington Palace). This had remained a plain space since the time of Mary II, in complete contrast to the King's Staircase. Kent painted the walls with a series of *trompe l'œil* niches and half-domed spaces with classical sculptures in them, and the Garter star and royal ciphers within the ceiling scheme, but pride of place was given to Gerard van Honthorst's vast canvas, *Mercury Presenting the Liberal Arts to Apollo and Diana* (fig. 61), originally commissioned by Charles I for the Banqueting House at Whitehall.

*The palace gardens*

In George I's reign the gardens remained little altered from the time of Queen Anne. Henry Wise, who had been appointed Royal Gardener under her, generally maintained the *status quo*. His only significant change was to remove the Tijou screen from the end of the Privy Garden and to resite it beside the park. In 1728 Wise was succeeded by Charles Bridgeman, who followed the wishes of Queen Caroline in reducing the formality and increasing the naturalistic effects in the gardens. In the Privy Garden, for example, the elaborate beds were grassed over, although the gardeners continued to keep the topiary in trim.

It was in these gardens – celebrated in many prints and engravings – that the courtiers walked, gossiped and flirted (fig. 123). Bridgeman's tenure lasted ten years. He was succeeded at Hampton Court by George Lowe and then John Greening, but there were few notable changes other than an increasing use of the former Melon Ground immediately to the north of the palace as the works yards for the gardens (a function this area still performs). Real change came after 1764, in the next reign, when Lancelot Brown was appointed.

*A family affair*

The problem of inter-generational rivalry continued. Frederick commissioned a series of portrait groups of himself making music with his sisters by his court painter, Philippe Mercier, in 1733. One of these depicts the musical group in William III's Banqueting House at Hampton Court (fig. 122). It was little matter that Frederick did not care much for his sisters, as he cared still less for his parents. The

123. *Anthony Highmore,*
A Perspective View of the
East Front of Hampton Court
taken from the Park Gate,
1744, *showing clipped conical*
*yews and the gardens peopled*
*with visitors. At this time the*
*palace gardens were in the care*
*of George Lowe, who had been*
*appointed Royal Gardener*
*for Hampton Court after the*
*death of Charles Bridgeman*
*in 1738. Bridgeman had had*
*responsibility for all the royal*
*gardens but after his death each*
*royal palace was assigned its*
*own gardener. With the post*
*went the Master Gardener's*
*house in the Wilderness and*
*the use of a yard on Hampton*
*Court Green.*

Queen believed her son to be impotent, and when – after numerous false starts – the Prince of Wales married "the most decent and prudent" Augusta of Saxe-Gotha in 1737, the Queen doubted the reality of her daughter-in-law's first pregnancy. She told Walpole, "Sir Robert, we shall be catched. At her labour I positively will be [present] ... I will be sure it is her child."

Her son chose to disregard this, and the *dénouement* of this family saga was played out at Hampton Court Palace. On 31 July 1737, the Prince and Princess of Wales dined in state there with the King and Queen, but after dinner the Princess went into labour. As soon as the contractions started, the Prince rushed his wife away to St James's Palace. The 24-km (15-mile) carriage journey was a painful trial to the Princess and, since St James's Palace was shut up for the summer, the baby was born on a bed covered with tablecloths, "a little rat of a girl, about the bigness of a good large toothpick case". The other members of the royal family were unaware of this drama and played cards until bedtime. Roused at one in the morning, the Queen and her party sped from Hampton Court to St James's and arrived before dawn.

This event continued the downward spiral of the relationship between George and Frederick. Shunned by his parents, the Prince's rival court became a new focus of loyalty. "Popularity always makes me sick," the Queen said, "but Fritz's popularity makes me vomit." When the royal family and their attendants left Hampton Court at the end of that October in 1737 to return to St James's Palace, it was for the last time. The Queen was seriously ill with complications stemming from her own last pregnancy, and she died on 20 November.

*The end of royal occupation*
The King lived for another twenty-three years, but he never took the court back to Hampton Court in the summer again. He dined there occasionally when he was in the vicinity, especially when he visited his prized stables and horse stud in Home Park. Meanwhile, the palace began to attract visitors who paid the housekeeper a small sum to allow them to enjoy the splendours of its architecture and the magnificence of its collection of paintings and furniture. The very first guidebook to Hampton Court Palace was published in 1742, as the second volume of George Bickham's *Deliciae Britannicae*. The circuit Bickham prescribed remained the visitor route around the palace for the next 250 years, a period in which Hampton Court ceased to be an occupied royal residence and became a place for public enjoyment and private accommodation.

# The 'GRACE-and-*Favour*' Palace after 1760

Abandoned as a royal residence, from 1760 Hampton Court Palace becomes a set of 'grace-and-favour' residences. By the later eighteenth century the Tudor palace comes to be recognized as a major architectural work, and the process of restoration of the fabric begins.

*124. Amateur theatricals in the Great Hall of Hampton Court Palace in aid of the Princess Frederica of Hanover's proposed convalescent home, 1881. Princess Frederica of Hanover and her husband, Baron von Pawel Rammingen, occupied Apartment 39 from 1880 to 1898. With the proceeds from this and other events the Princess was able to open a home in East Molesey for women recuperating after a difficult childbirth.*

## George III's preferences

The second half of the palace's history, from 1760 to the present day, is one of increasing openness, first to new types of residents and then to the visiting public. This has been coupled with a growing recognition of its important position in the history of English architecture. With the early death of Frederick, Prince of Wales in 1752 the succession passed to his son George, who became George III in 1760 at his grandfather's death. The new King received the news at Kew – which was to have its own place in the history of royal building and residence in the next forty years – but Hampton Court Palace was now effectively abandoned as a viable royal dwelling. There is a tradition that George II lost his temper at Hampton Court with his grandson, striking Prince George and instilling in him the dislike he felt for the palace ever afterwards. The story is barely plausible, since the two would not have been there at the same time unless one of the old King's occasional summer visits had coincided with a rare sojourn by the young Prince. Whatever the reason, both Hampton Court Palace and Kensington Palace seemed tainted by their associations with past family unhappiness, and George III chose not to live in either of them.

George bought Buckingham House (to be called the Queen's House and later Buckingham Palace) as a domestic alternative to the formality and antiquated arrangements of St James's Palace, the sovereign's official London residence. Among the many treasures raided from Hampton Court Palace and brought to the Queen's House were the Raphael cartoons. They were hung in the new Saloon in December 1763. When fire broke out in outbuildings at Hampton Court in 1770, the King said that he would not have been sorry if the whole place had burned down. His attention turned instead to Windsor Castle, which had been little regarded by the royal family for sixty years, and it became once again the principal royal retreat outside London. In the last years before his

*125. Lancelot 'Capability' Brown by John Sherwin after Nathaniel Dance (c. 1769). As the royal gardener he was entitled to live in Wilderness House, to the north of the palace.*

The eminent scientist Sir Michael Faraday, a grace-and-favour resident at Hampton Court, advised on the proposed removal of the Raphael cartoons to South Kensington in 1865. Although of the opinion that they should stay, he was overruled.

Queen Adelaide was granted Bushy House as a residence after the death of William IV in 1837 and lived there until her own death in 1849.

In the late nineteenth century an old sedan chair, known as 'the Push', was used by the palace residents for moving around the building.

126. *John Spyers,* The East View of the Second Inferior Court, c. 1780. *Master Carpenter's Court looking east. The windows and chimneys show the progressive 'Georgianization' of the building although service areas like this remained relatively untouched. Spyers's views are an incomparable guide to the appearance of both palace and gardens in the later eighteenth century on the eve of the major programme of restoration that turned the building back to an idealized view of its Tudor appearance.*

127. *John Spyers,* The Middle of the Wilderness Garden at Hampton Court, c. 1780. *The Maze has been a source of delight and consternation to visitors from Daniel Defoe to Jerome K. Jerome and Paddington Bear.*

128. *John Spyers,* A View of the Green House Garden, taken at the Green House Gate, c. 1780. *This is the Privy Garden looking south, after Lancelot 'Capability' Brown had been permitted to allow the trees to grow naturally out of their clipped shape.*

death in 1820 Windsor was the place of incarceration for the senile, 'mad' King (his unpredictable behaviour was caused by the hereditary disease of porphyria).

Although his visits to Hampton Court were rare, George III interested himself considerably in the palace's affairs and ensured that the building was properly maintained. For example, Verrio's mural paintings on the King's Staircase were restored at the King's insistence in 1781. Eleven years before, he had approved the plans by the Office of Works for the major remodelling by Sir William Chambers of the Great Gatehouse on the West Front, necessitated by its highly unstable structural condition. One of the glories of Wolsey's palace, the towering brick edifice was reduced in height by two storeys. Chambers made the central part of the tower (previously flanked by much taller turrets with domes) into the highest element in the new design. That was topped by a new pierced parapet in a gothic idiom (a difficult medium for a classical architect to bring off).

*Garden changes*

Meanwhile, Lancelot 'Capability' Brown (fig. 125), who had been made Head Gardener at Hampton Court in 1764, had royal blessing for his policies. He retained the layout and structure of the palace gardens instead of sweeping away the older formality as he did in other places, but allowed a more naturalistic form to emerge. He achieved that simply by no longer cutting the topiary. The result may have seemed more natural to him, but to many visitors it just looked unkempt (fig. 128).

Brown's most famous and most lasting contribution was to plant the Great Vine in 1768, which has long been one of the biggest attractions at the palace (fig. 131). A cutting from an already old Black Hamburgh grape at Valentines, Essex, the Great Vine was given its own vinehouse in the south-west corner of the Pond Gardens. (This has since been extended or rebuilt on various occasions as the vine has grown, the last time being in 1964.) Even thirty years after it was planted, its branches had already filled the allotted space, 24 yards long by 6 yards wide (22 x 5.5 m), and yielded 1800 bunches of grapes.

## Palace residents

George III and his wife, Charlotte of Mecklenburg-Strelitz, came to Hampton Court from time to time. They visited former courtiers who resided there, going several times in 1768, and the King held occasional audiences in the State Apartments throughout his reign. There were further rounds of royal visits after 1795, to William V, Prince of Orange. A cousin of the King, the Prince had been forced to flee from The Netherlands ahead of the French Revolutionary armies. He was granted the use of apartments on the East Front of the palace, together with the Queen's Guard and Presence Chambers on the floor above. A figure of fun for his rotund shape and his amorous activities (fig. 129), the Prince of Orange was able to return to his homeland after the Peace of Amiens in 1802.

The Prince was by no means the only person to live at Hampton Court, although he had a more

129. *William V of Orange's busy pursuit of the opposite sex caricatured in an etching published in 1796 by H. Humphrey:* The Orangerie; – or – the Dutch Cupid reposing, After the Fatigues of Planting. *Lord Holland wrote, "When the Prince of Orange resided at Hampton Court, his amours with the servant-maids were supposed to be very numerous."*

privileged and better appointed home than others. In the 1740s, a select group of courtiers had been given the privilege of residing there in the summer months. Some of them were relatively poor. From this stemmed the practice of residence "by the grace and favour" of the sovereign, in which the palace was divided into a series of apartments for those deserving of assistance. Beginning formally in 1767 and organized under official warrants from 1773, the practice lasted almost to the close of the twentieth century.

## 'Grace and favour'

In the first instance these grace-and-favour residents were members of the court with good connections. Hannah More, the moralizing author, noted on a visit in 1770 that "the private apartments are almost full, they are occupied by people of fashion, mostly of quality". William Brummell, the father of 'Beau'

Brummell (the king of fashionable Bath), was among them and he occupied an apartment from 1772. Dr Samuel Johnson was famously refused an apartment four years later, on the grounds that the waiting list was now full. This practice shifted by degrees, until the palace became by the 1840s almost exclusively the residence of widows whose husbands had served with distinction in military or imperial service but who had often fallen on harder times.

Over the course of time, the palace was divided into more than fifty grace-and-favour apartments; some were dozens of rooms in extent, others much smaller. A parliamentary review in 1842 recorded between sixty and seventy households in the palace and its attendant buildings, with 150 to 200 servants between them. Only a few years before, William IV had called his near-forgotten palace "the quality poorhouse". Charles Dickens characterized the residents as "civilized gypsies" in his novel *Little Dorrit* (1857):

There was a temporary air about their establishments, as if they were going away the moment they could get anything better; there was also a dissatisfied air about themselves, as if they took it very ill that they had not already got something better .... Mental reservations and artful mysteries grew out of these things. Callers, looking steadily into the eyes of their receivers, pretended not to smell cooking three feet off; people, confronting closets accidentally left open, pretended not to see bottles; visitors, with their heads against a partition of thin canvas and a page and a young female at high words on the other side, made believe to be sitting in a primeval silence. There was no end to

LEFT 132. *The 1882 fire at Hampton Court, as graphically reported in* the Illustrated London News, 23 *December 1882. The fire broke out in a grace-and-favour apartment above the Queen's Gallery. One servant died and several rooms were burnt or damaged. An enquiry followed, held in the palace with a jury comprising fifteen palace residents and the Chaplain as foreman. The cause of the fire was found to be "the overflowing of the burning spirit in a small spirit lamp". Fires were an ever-present danger, but also offered the opportunity to replace damaged buildings in an appropriate Tudor style.*

BELOW 133. *The 'painted room' in the Banqueting House in 1936 during the occupation of Mrs Mary Campbell. After her death in 1945, the Banqueting House was opened to the public. Earlier residents had ensured that the paintings, which depicted naked figures of the gods, were covered up with bookcases or fabric to spare their blushes.*

the social-accommodation bills of this nature which the gypsies of gentility were constantly drawing upon, and accepting for, one another.

Despite their size and seeming grandeur, these apartments often lacked basic amenities such as water closets, sewage, kitchens located within easy reach of dining rooms, and, later, gas and electricity. Slowly the palace was brought closer to contemporary living standards, although even as late as the mid-twentieth century a 105-year-old resident was refused permission to install a bathroom. Not only were there complaints and disputes about amenities between residents and the relevant authorities – the Lord Chamberlain and the Board of Works being the main ones – but also friction over subjects such as rank and precedence. There was continuing rancour over the seating arrangements within the Chapel Royal, the keeping of pets, the use of the gardens and relations with the growing bands of paying visitors.

Of these, the greatest difficulties were in the Chapel. Seating for the worshippers was strictly by rank and social standing, policed by the resident housekeeper. There was sometimes unseemly behaviour when elderly ladies tried to pull rank over their neighbours or over the visitors who tried to come into the Chapel. The problem of seating had become so urgent that in 1866 the architect Anthony Salvin reordered the pews and added a block of box pews in the centre. Even with these enhancements the disputes continued, until the Lord Chamberlain decreed that no longer were those attending services in the Chapel to sit by rank.

Pets were a cause of serious friction between residents and the housekeeper. In 1880 the residents petitioned the Lord Chamberlain to change the rule that dogs were not allowed to be kept in the palace. As a concession, he permitted the keeping of 'lap dogs'. This definition, however, was widely exploited as ladies gave promises that their lap dog – perhaps a German shepherd or golden retriever – was extremely well behaved.

Occasional rogues as well as the families of daring explorers and devoted servants of Empire occupied the apartments. Lord and Lady Henry Gordon, who lived in an apartment overlooking Fountain Court

TOP 134. *Intrepid Edwardian ladies climbing on to the roof of the Great Hall in September 1905. This photograph is taken from an album belonging to Madeleine Keyes, daughter of Lady Keyes who was resident in Apartment 30 from 1902 to 1916. Madeleine's sister Dorothea Agnes (Lady Gough) was married in the Chapel Royal in June 1907 and was later a resident in the palace herself from 1934 to 1954.*

ABOVE 135. *Princesses Bamba and Catherine Duleep Singh, the two eldest daughters of the Maharaja Duleep Singh, who were granted tenancy of Faraday House with their sister Sophia in 1896. On their arrival, they discovered they would have to share the Chapel gallery seats in the Royal Pew and decided they would have nothing more to do with the Chapel Royal. Later, both became notable members of the suffragette movement in the years of women's struggle for the vote before the First World War.*

from 1850, were constantly being reprimanded for misconduct. In 1854, for example, Lady Gordon allowed water to pour through the floor, which seeped behind pictures in the Queen's Private Apartments; in 1857 she was rebuked for lighting a fire near trees in Home Park whilst having a picnic; and in 1864 her daughters were threatened with prosecution for picking rhododendrons in the Wilderness. The family's fortunes worsened; in 1865 Lord Gordon was declared bankrupt and bailiffs seized almost all of the family's furniture. Lord Gordon disappeared but Lady Gordon and her family took refuge in another apartment for two years before she died.

Miss Baly, a new grace-and-favour resident of the Banqueting House in the south gardens in 1864, was horrified to find that the rooms were decorated with naked figures (fig. 133). She wrote to the Lord Chamberlain, "I find very objectionable the large undressed figures in the frescoes on each side of the fireplace and venture to suggest that they should be either draped or clouded in such a manner as render them appropriate decorations for a drawing room." Her wish was granted, and only in 1945 were the Baroque wall paintings uncovered once more.

The famous Antarctic explorer Sir Robert Falcon Scott was married in the Chapel Royal in 1908; his bride, Kathleen Bruce, a famous sculptor in her own right, was living in a grace-and-favour apartment at the time with her aunt, Mrs Zoë Thomson. In 1915 a grace-and-favour warrant was granted to Scott's mother, Hannah, until her death in 1924. Some years later the same apartment was allocated to Emily, the widow of the Antarctic explorer Sir Ernest Shackleton, who lived there from 1930 until she died in 1936.

Minor royal residents continued to come to live in the palace. Elizabeth Emily FitzClarence, one of ten illegitimate children fathered by William IV before he came to the throne, lived on the ground floor of the East Front of the palace in the 1830s. In the 1880s another resident was Princess Frederica of Hanover, a descendant of George II. Following the early death of her daughter, she founded a home nearby for poor and delicate married women recovering from childbirth, for which she held fund-raising evenings of entertainment in the Great Hall (fig. 124). She also made the last major addition to the built fabric of the palace: an extension of her apartments, situated in the south-west corner.

More exotic were various of the children of Maharajah Duleep Singh, the Sikh leader who had been brought to Britain as a boy in 1849 after the Second Anglo-Sikh War. Princess Sophia Duleep Singh and other members of her immediate family (fig. 135) lived in Faraday House, opposite Hampton Court Green. A prominent suffragette, she often went on protest demonstrations in the years before the First World War. Others involved in the struggle

ABOVE 136. *A reproduction Tudor room in Lady Baden-Powell's apartment annexe, 1976. The three-storey annexe filled the western half of the Great Kitchens and was dismantled in 1978. The Tudor room was later reconstructed in an exhibition behind the colonnade in Clock Court relating the history of the palace.*

RIGHT 137. *Field Marshal Viscount Wolseley, the victor of the Zulu Wars, photographed in Apartment 39, c. 1910. He resided in the palace from 1899 to his death in 1913; his widow transformed the apartment into a memorial to him.*

for the vote threatened to bring their fight to the palace. In February 1913 Hampton Court was closed to the public for seven months "owing to the fear of damage by women suffragists" and extra policemen were posted on guard. In the 1930s the Princess wrote to the Lord Chamberlain's office requesting certain improvements, including the installation of electricity. This was ironic, as a previous grace-and-favour tenant of the same house had been Michael Faraday, whose research had laid the foundations of the exploitation of electricity.

In 1936 a Russian royal refugee came to live at the palace with her family. The Grand Duchess Xenia Alexandra was the sister of the assassinated Tsar Nicholas II and widow of Alexander Michael, Grand Duke of Russia. She remained in Wilderness House, close to the Maze, until her death in 1960. Among the best-known twentieth-century residents until the 1960s was Olave, Lady Baden-Powell, widow of the founder of the Boy Scouts and herself the head of the Girl Guides movement. No stranger to the palace, since her friend Lady Manning already occupied a forty-room apartment on the West Front, Lady

Baden-Powell was given an apartment in 1942, as her own home had been commandeered "for the duration" of the Second World War. Aged fifty-three, she was the youngest grace-and-favour resident. Past and present Girl Guides from all over the world came to see her there. Her sixteen-room apartment (fig. 136) extended from the Great Hall northwards and incorporated significant parts of Henry VIII's Great Kitchens. One huge fireplace had even been converted into a bathroom. As Lady Baden-Powell herself noted in her autobiography, her bedroom beside the Great Hall was said to have been Shakespeare's players' dressing-room when they performed there in 1604 and 1605, "so I never

ABOVE 138. *The corridor of Apartment 21 on the first floor of the west range in 1937. Mrs Barbara Cecil Brooke was living there at the time. Following her death in 1979 the apartment was home to the Textile Conservation Centre from 1982 to 1999. This is a rare view of the interior of a grace-and-favour apartment.*

RIGHT 139. *W.J. Bennet after Charles Wild,* Gothic Hall (the Great Hall) *from W.H. Pyne's* Royal Residences *(1817–20). The Tudor hall, stripped of its fittings as a theatre, is revealed once more. The gothic doorway in the east wall was inserted by Wyatt to replace its eighteenth-century predecessor. New flagstones were laid on the floor and the walls were plastered to look like ancient stonework.*

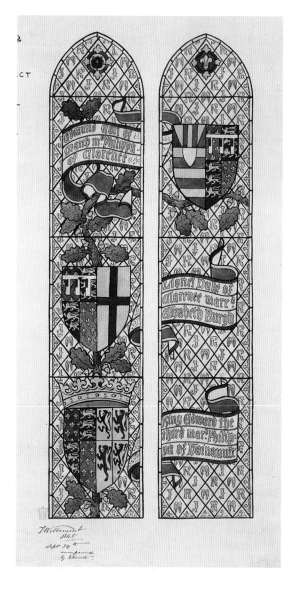

know whether Shakespeare dresses in my bedroom or whether I sleep in his dressing-room!" Lady Baden-Powell feared she would rapidly be forgotten,

> ... as I grow older and drop out of the public eye ... At the foot of my stairs, a small boy was spelling out my name on the name-plate. His mother yanked him away impatiently. "Come along," she said. "It's no good reading that. She's been dead for years."

A few palace residents remain, but the practice of granting new tenancies ceased in 1969. The legacy continues to this day, not least in the name-plates, bells, deliveries baskets and door numbers that survive in almost every corner, as well as the staff that live in the palace, including the Vine Keeper, Head Gardener and Chaplain.

## Rediscovering the Antique

The long saga of grace-and-favour residence was played out against the story of works and architectural discovery at Hampton Court Palace. Anthony

Salvin, who worked in the Chapel Royal in the late 1860s to solve the residents' seating problems, was but one architect of distinction who was employed there. A roll call of English architects and designers left their mark. They followed in the footsteps of Sir William Chambers, Surveyor of the King's Works. He had been the King's Drawing Master when George III was a prince but was supplanted in his affections by James Wyatt in the 1790s. When Chambers had essayed the gothic style, on the Great Gatehouse, it had been half-hearted. Wyatt and his Clerk of Works Thomas Hardwick embraced the ancient style with enthusiasm and began the lengthy process of turning the clock back at the palace, uncovering and restoring earlier fabric. On the King's orders in 1800, Wyatt removed the theatre from the Great Hall, revealing the Tudor interior that had not been seen for a century (fig. 139). In this work, Wyatt began the process of making the Great Hall even more Tudor than it had ever been, by opening a new doorway from the dais into the Great Watching Chamber in an exemplary copy of the arched doorway in the adjacent Horn Room. There are several 'snapshots' of the palace (and of other royal homes) at exactly this time in the evocative series of watercolours commissioned for W.H. Pyne's *Royal Residences*, published in 1817–20. This was the point at which Hampton Court was on the cusp of change.

One of the dominant themes of Hampton Court Palace in the nineteenth century was the rediscovery of Tudor architecture. Effort was directed to putting back the Tudor elements which had been lost, and sometimes embellishing them further. The architecture of the sixteenth century had come to seem debased, having neither the full glory of the medieval Gothic nor the purity of the revived classical style. In the opening decades of the nineteenth century this attitude changed and Hampton Court was in part both the cause and the beneficiary. A.C. Pugin's *Specimens of Gothic Architecture* (1821–23) contained the first detailed measured drawings of the Great Hall and its roof, while Joseph Nash began the romanticizing of the Tudor court in its proper setting in the illustrations to his *The Mansions of England in the Olden Time* (1839–48; see fig. 6).

### Edward Jesse's influence
William IV (1830–1837) succeeded his brother George IV (1820–1830), whose main effect on the palace had been to strip the gardens of much of their statuary. From that date the antiquarian approach to Hampton Court took firm hold. Edward Jesse, who was appointed Itinerant Deputy Surveyor in the Office of Woods, Forests and Land Revenues in 1834, had a particular and lasting effect on the palace over the succeeding twenty years.

142. The Entrance to
Hampton Court Palace,
*Woolnoth after J.P. Neale, 1814.*
*Many of the Georgian sash*
*windows were soon to be*
*comprehensively replaced in the*
*great campaign of 'Tudorization'*
*that was intended to return*
*the palace to its supposed*
*appearance in its heyday.*

With a deep romanticism and affection for gothic styles and picturesque irregularity – and with an equally deep distaste for Wren and the Baroque – Jesse supervised a series of restorations and re-presentations. The most notable was that of the Great Hall itself (fig. 140). Left clear and relatively bare by Wyatt, it was transformed between 1840 and 1846 into a state that Jesse believed Cardinal Wolsey and Henry VIII would have recognized instantly. The great series of Abraham tapestries, one of the glories to have survived from Henry VIII's reign, was returned there from the King's State Apartments. The hammerbeam ceiling was repainted and the windows of both the Great Hall and the Great Watching Chamber were filled with stained glass to the designs of Thomas Willement. Heraldic badges and figures in the glass evoked the genealogy of Henry VIII's wives (fig. 141), of the King and his family, and of his Chancellor, Thomas Wolsey. Artful arrangements of arms and armour were placed around the walls on specially constructed corbels, and deer antlers (all from the parks) were added for further effect. When Jesse had finished, it was "probably the finest and most brilliantly embellished building in Europe", in the words of the correspondent of the *Gentleman's Magazine.*

Jesse continued in the same manner wherever he had opportunity. The ceiling of the Chapel Royal was repainted in its original rich blue colouring and gilded with gold stars. (The ceiling had been painted white in the reign of Queen Anne.) The design was

further enhanced with mottoes. With Edward Blore as supervising architect, considerable changes were made to the palace exterior in the course of the 1840s. First the West Front and then its projecting wings were returned to their original appearance by the replacement of Georgian sash windows with Tudor-style casements (fig. 142). Success here – for the restoration was universally acclaimed – was followed by similar programmes of work in Clock Court, Base Court and Master Carpenter's Court.

Attention then turned to the decayed and miscellaneous collection of chimneys. These too were replaced, often in more fantastic shapes than had ever been there originally but based on surviving examples found at other sixteenth-century English houses. Only the brighter brick distinguished much of this Victorian work from the original; the mortar was artificially blackened with ash and soot, to match the now discoloured Tudor mortar (leaving problems that are still being resolved in the present day).

The impetus behind all this work was not simply the result of a successful antiquarian campaign, and it was certainly not done to please the growing grace-and-favour resident population. As the public were admitted from 1838, the privileged few were replaced by the many. They were all keen not only to see the gardens, the magnificent art collection and the State Apartments but also the considerably more romantic Tudor parts of the palace. Visitor demand and antiquarian romance coincided. In many ways, they still do.

# The VISITOR'S Hampton COURT from 1838

Opened to public view in 1838, the palace becomes one of the great tourist attractions of the nineteenth century. The process of rediscovery and restoration in both palace and gardens continues.

*143. Detail of a London Transport poster by Clive Gardiner, 1927, one of many from the 1900s to the 1950s advertising the delights of Hampton Court. The system of buses, trams and trolley-buses brought the great majority of visitors in the inter-war years.*

## Visitors and tourists

In 1838, in an early act of generosity towards her public, the young Queen Victoria (1837–1901), niece of George IV and William IV, ordered that Hampton Court Palace "should be thrown open to all her subjects without restriction". It seemed simple enough, but there was not universal rejoicing. In the eighteenth century and even earlier, visitors of social standing had been admitted on payment of a fee to the resident housekeeper, who conducted them around at some speed, pointing out Old Master paintings and artefacts such as Cardinal Wolsey's supposed (and oversized) shoe. This new direction smacked of democracy.

The spirit of revolution was still abroad in Europe. Some commentators had visions "of an insulting rabble, such as that which invaded the Tuileries in the time of Louis XVI, marching through the State Apartments, tearing down the tapestries, wrecking the furniture, and carrying off pictures". The grace-and-favour residents were also unhappy. Ernest Law – who dominated the palace and its presentation to the public at the end of the nineteenth century and the start of the twentieth – later wrote that this body of "decayed nobles and court pensioners" feared the loss of "the immunity they had hitherto enjoyed from the more objectionable accompaniments inseparable from crowds of noisy excursionists and trippers". The apprehensions about revolutionaries were ill-founded, although the resident population

did come to feel under siege from those who began to arrive in great numbers to see both palace and gardens. Hundreds of thousands were visiting each year by the middle of the nineteenth century. In 175 years the flow of visitors has never ceased (fig. 147).

### Writers and guides

The palace was a "well-loved resort of Cockneydom", in the words of the novelist Anthony Trollope. Sunday was the favoured day, when house and grounds were frequently overrun. William Howitt, a travel and country writer of the third quarter of the nineteenth century, thought that Hampton Court was "one of the bravest pleasures that a party of happy friends can promise themselves. Especially as it is calculated to charm the thousands of pleasure-seekers from the dense and dusty vastness of London."

The most celebrated nineteenth-century fictional visitors to the palace were Jerome K. Jerome's *Three Men in a Boat* of 1889. In the novel, Harris recounted to his two companions – not forgetting the dog, Montmorency – the story of a previous visit when he and a group of others became hopelessly lost in the Maze (then, as now, one of the principal attractions in the palace grounds) (fig. 144):

They picked up various other people who wanted to get it over, as they went along, until they absorbed all the persons in the maze. People who had given up all hopes of either getting in or out,

---

In 1876 Vincent van Gogh visited Hampton Court. He wrote to his brother shortly after, praising the paintings and the "beautiful gardens and long avenues of chestnut and lime trees".

In the late nineteenth century the Maze was described as "rather dilapidated with much use". It was replanted in 1908 and again in 1932 and 1963.

Edward Jesse was appointed a magistrate to deal with troublemakers who came to Hampton Court and were in the habit of committing "depredations on the gardens".

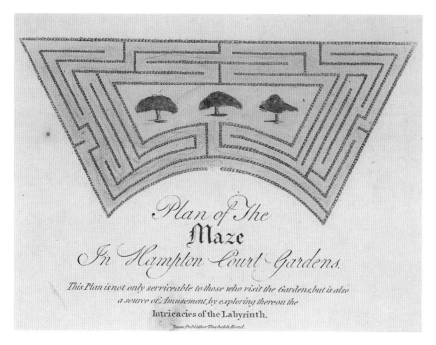

Plan of The

Maze

In Hampton Court Gardens.

This Plan is not only serviceable to those who visit the Gardens, but is also
a source of Amusement, by exploring thereon the
Intricacies of the Labyrinth.

Snow, Publisher Theobalds Road.

144. A souvenir plan of the
Maze, one of the great draws
for visitors to the palace gardens
since the eighteenth century and
a scene of frequent frustration.
The annotation beneath the
plan reads: "This Plan is not
only serviceable to those who
visit the Gardens, but is also
a source of Amusement by
exploring thereon the Intricacies
of the Labyrinth".

or of ever seeing their home and friends again, picked up courage at the sight of Harris and his party, and joined the procession, blessing him .... "That map may be all right enough," said one of the party, "if you know whereabouts we are in it now."

Harris didn't know, and suggested that the best thing to do would be to go back to the entrance, and begin again. For the beginning again part of it there was not much enthusiasm; but with regard to the advisability of going back to the entrance there was complete unanimity, and so they turned, and trailed after Harris again, in the opposite direction. About ten minutes more passed and then they found themselves in the centre.

Harris thought at first of pretending that that was what he was aiming at; but the crowd looked dangerous, and he decided to treat it as an accident.

Finally, after many more vain attempts, the party called for help, but the young keeper who came in to fetch them out got lost himself and only when a more experienced keeper returned from lunch was the party released at last.

This famous humorous episode may be balanced by another passage in Jerome's description of the visit, which celebrates the antique beauty of the place:

What a dear old wall that is that runs along by the river there! I never pass it without feeling better for the sight of it. Such a mellow, sweet, bright old wall .... There are fifty shades and tints and hues in every ten yards of that old wall .... I've often thought I should like to live at Hampton Court. It looks so peaceful and so quiet, and it is such a dear old place to ramble round in the early morning before many people are about.

145. The Blue Border in the
East Front gardens, depicted
in 1913. By the late nineteenth
century the palace gardens had
become famous for their brightly
coloured flower borders and
carpet bedding. Ernest Law
wrote in 1926: "There are no
gardens in England where
the modern developments in
bedding out and the planting of
herbaceous and mixed borders
have been carried out to so high
a pitch as at Hampton Court.
Indeed, to a great extent, the
fashion was started here."

Guidebooks were available to visitors from the 1740s, and increased in number when the palace was opened fully to the public. Edward Jesse not only supervised works in the palace but also wrote hugely successful guides. *Gleanings in Natural History* appeared in 1835, *A Summer's Day at Hampton Court* four years later. The first was concerned more with natural phenomena, and particular pride of place was given to the giant Cardinal spiders that are peculiar to the palace and its park. The second gave detailed itineraries to and from central London as well as descriptions of the principal attractions at and around the palace. John Grundy's *The Stranger's Guide* followed in 1843; it went through many editions and became the standard guide of the middle decades of the century.

*Transport and amenities*

Increased leisure time and improved transport spurred the growth in nineteenth-century tourism. An astonishing total of ten million visitors had come to the palace by 1881, sped there by new forms of transport as well as by curiosity. In the 1830s the horse-drawn omnibus departed from central London every twenty minutes. In 1849 the London and South-Western Railway opened its branch line to Hampton Court, terminating at Sir William Tite's neo-Jacobean station building. In the early twentieth century, visitors could come from Hammersmith by tram, and later by trolley-bus (fig. 143). There were

HAMPTON COURT PALACE
THE BLUE BORDER

always river trips available, and the rise of the motor omnibus and subsequently the private car made Hampton Court increasingly accessible to all (fig. 146).

An increasing range of facilities was available to visitors: lavatories and a small shop had been added within the palace by the 1870s, while nine hotels and two restaurants were established at the gates. The dining rooms in one hotel could seat 500. As it became ever easier to visit Hampton Court, with improved and increasingly affordable transport, the 1871 Bank Holiday Act gave new occasions for visiting. It was also held responsible for a widely deplored increase in "rowdy and bawdy behaviour". In the 1880s palace residents were complaining that indecent bathing in the river added to their burden from visitors, although a Metropolitan Police report of 1884 stated that "nude bathing is only an offence if there is an intention to insult". By the close of the century, complaints about the "loose women" who gathered around the soldiers quartered in the Barrack Block beside Trophy Gate were becoming legion.

The peak times for visitors coincided particularly with the displays of flowers in the gardens and parks: horse chestnuts, daffodils, tulips or rhododendrons. Ernest Law observed Sunday visitors "full of high spirits, intent on enjoying themselves", and he approved of "men rationally dressed in easy shooting suits or flannels, and girls in neat and pretty lawn-tennis or boating costumes ... treading the velvet turf and scenting the flowers" and otherwise enjoying the outdoor pleasures of the grounds (fig. 148).

## Interior displays

Inside the palace, the considerable wear and tear on the buildings from the tide of visitors meant that various changes needed to be made from the 1850s. There was comprehensive reflooring in the most heavily trafficked areas with tiles and other more durable but inauthentic materials. Metal barriers and even grilles were erected to protect vulnerable pictures and furnishings (fig. 149).

There were always many visitors who came to enjoy the treasured paintings hanging on the walls. Gradually, the palace had become a crowded art

TOP RIGHT 146. *Private cars parked on the West Front approach in 1928. The pressure for parking space is nothing new. To remove this eyesore and to protect the building, a new car park was opened behind the Barrack Block in the 1930s.*

CENTRE 147. *The throng of visitors in Base Court c. 1936, including some who appear to have taken a dip in the Thames before arriving.*

RIGHT 148. *Indian visitors in Home Park in 1902, when a large contingent from the Indian Army was encamped there. A military presence in and around the palace lasted until the Second World War.*

When Queen Victoria opened up the palace to all, Law wrote, "the thirty-two rooms of the state apartments exhibited a strange heterogeneous conglomeration of a thousand pictures of every value, of every period and of every school, hung up anyhow and everywhere, just as they came". A considerable part of the work undertaken during the course of the nineteenth century, and since, has been to return the palace and its contents to order.

Among the most glorious of the palace's treasures had been the Raphael cartoons for the tapestry series of the *Acts of the Apostles*. Taken to the Queen's House in 1763, they were returned to Hampton Court in 1804. When the palace opened to the general public they were one of the high points of the tour. The constant moving of the fragile cartoons was seen as a threat to their survival and in 1865 they were removed in massive crates by the Royal Engineers to the Victoria and Albert Museum in South Kensington, where they still hang (fig. 150). This was part of a controversial deal struck with the museum's founder, Henry Cole. The museum had acquired piecemeal a variety of objects from the palace, including the majority of the great ironwork screen by Tijou. Most of these were returned in due course, but Cole's prize acquisition of the cartoon series remains.

Richard Redgrave, Surveyor of the Royal Pictures and a close friend of Cole, took the opportunity to undertake a major reorganization of the paintings at Hampton Court in the course of the 1860s. The Mantegna *Triumphs of Caesar* paintings were moved to the Communication Gallery, where special floor traps were installed for their swift removal in the event of fire. Major discoveries were made on the

ABOVE 149. *Protective grilles around furniture in the Queen's Audience Chamber, photographed in the 1920s or earlier. Although security measures were and are a necessity, in many parts of the palace the late Victorian arrangements seem excessive to the modern eye.*

RIGHT 150. *One of the Royal Engineers' crates used for transporting the Raphael cartoons from Hampton Court to the Victoria and Albert Museum in 1865. When it became known that the cartoons were to be moved to South Kensington, the inhabitants of Hampton Court drew up a petition to the House of Lords demanding that the cartoons stay, but to no avail. The precious objects were moved with great care, the "case containing the Cartoons being suspended in its van 'by india rubber springs'".*

gallery as much as, if not more than, a historic house. The changes in a century and a half were described by Ernest Law in his 1902 handbook to the paintings. The palace's original collection of some two hundred works

remained undisturbed during the long reign of George III. The public were then admitted in batches, and walked round the rooms attended by the housekeeper, who pointed out the pictures with a long stick, calling out, at the same time, the roll of names in a loud voice to the awe-stricken visitors. They seem to have been pretty equally divided between Raphael, Giorgione, Titian and Holbein. But in the reigns of George IV and William IV considerable changes were made, and a great many pictures from Kensington Palace, Carlton House, Buckingham House and Windsor Castle, some of them of much beauty and interest but many of them little better than rubbish, were sent to swell the contents of Wolsey's palace.

151. The 'bed museum' in the
Queen's Private Dining Room:
left to right, Queen Caroline's
state bed, George II's travelling
bed and William III's state
bed. One of the features of the
twentieth-century trend for
more authentic and appropriate
room presentation was to return
furnishings to the setting for
which they were intended.
These beds were all placed in
more appropriate settings during
the major re-presentation of
the 1930s.

way: the Alexander tapestries in the Queen's Gallery
were uncovered from beneath papered linen. Alongside these changes there was a considerable
reordering of the furnishings, making the interior
more of a museum and less of a palace. In a series of
restorations, tapestries were removed from walls of
the State Apartments to other rooms. The collections
were grouped and regrouped on didactic rather than
historical principles. The Queen's Private Dining
Room became a bed museum, containing Queen
Caroline's state bed, George II's travelling bed and
William III's state bed all in a row (fig. 151).

*Ghosts*

Little by little public interest grew in both the antiquity
of palace and contents, and the beauty and accessi-
bility of gardens and grounds. In his 1897 book on
Hampton Court, William Holden Hunt described the
palace's dual appeal. It was a "holiday-ground for thousands of Londoners" who were "orderly folk, merry,
and not very attentive to historical association or even
natural beauty". It was also a "world invisible or half
known" filled with history where "imagination and
tradition vie in bringing forth tales of strange noises
and mysterious presences".

The best-selling picture postcards of Hampton
Court in the decades around 1900 were of ghostly
spectres in various of the historic spaces (fig. 152). It
was little matter that these were obvious fakes; the
palace famously had ghosts and these images were
as close as most visitors would get to any evidence for
them. The legend of the ghost of Queen Catherine
Howard, eternally rushing along the Haunted
Gallery to plead for her life, was the best-known
example, but ectoplasmic encounters were expected
around every corner. Although no ghost postcards

152. A typical postcard of 'The
Hampton Court Palace Ghost'
in the Great Hall. The ghost
of Catherine Howard "is said
to be seen at night rushing
through the Great Hall. She
stops suddenly, and wringing
her hands shrieks despairingly,
then returns and disappears
at the entrance to the haunted
chamber."

are on sale today, interest in the spectral presences at
the palace continues almost unabated. When a possible ghost was captured on a closed-circuit television
camera in 2003, the news went round the world.

**Restoration**

The closing decades of the nineteenth century witnessed not only popular interest in palace ghosts but
also renewed attention to the fabric and the grounds.
The architect John Lessels worked on the restoration
of both Hampton Court Palace and Windsor Castle,
and gave them a reinforced Tudor and a medieval
appearance respectively. The most publicly prominent of Lessels's works at Hampton Court were the
extensive repairs to Anne Boleyn's Gateway and the
Tudor Astronomical Clock, which was provided with
a new mechanism in 1879, the grassing over of Base
Court and the restoration of the Great Gatehouse in
1882. The western entrance, shorn of its upper
storeys a century before, was given its present-day
appearance with new shafts framing Sir William
Chambers's central parapet. A new stone vault
designed on the best antiquarian principles incorporating the arms of Queen Victoria and Cardinal
Wolsey spanned the entrance arch (fig. 153). The final
touch was added when the original wooden doors
were found and put back in their rightful place; they
were discovered to have spent the previous hundred
years as the floor of the palace carpenter's workshop.

**The Hampton Court Palace Ghost.**
The Ghost of Catherine Howard, wife of Henry VIII. said to be seen at night rushing through the Great Hall. She stops suddenly, and wringing her hands shrieks
despairingly, then returns and disappears at the entrance to the haunted chamber.

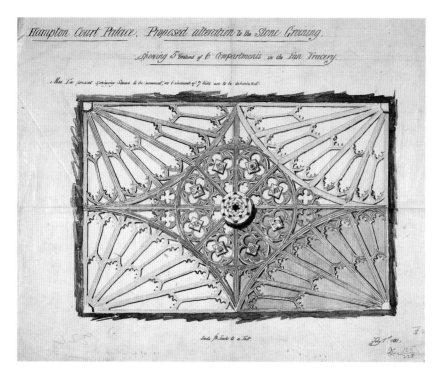

Hampton Court Palace, Proposed alteration to the Stone Groining.

Showing 5 instead of 6 Compartments in the Fan Tracery.

153. Proposal for alteration
to the stone groining in the
Great Gatehouse vault, 1881.
Chambers had removed the
original Tudor vault from the
archway when the gatehouse
was overhauled in 1771–73.
The new vault inserted in 1882
was designed by Lessels and
approved by the College of Arms.

154. *Design for the Knot Garden
by Ernest Law, 1924. Law had
already designed a similar
garden for Shakespeare's house
at Stratford-upon-Avon. He
claimed that at Hampton Court
the new garden was laid out on
"an ugly, shapeless plot, partly
gravelled and partly planted
with evergreens, lilacs, etc, in a
straggling bed". For over thirty
years his influence extended to
every aspect of the palace, its
history and decoration.*

Fire was a constant danger. The damage to rooms above the Queen's Gallery from a domestic fire in 1882 (fig. 132) paled into insignificance compared with the destruction of some seventy-five rooms on the north front four years later. This provided an opportunity for Lessels to replace them with work even more clearly Tudor than what had been there before. A total of forty well-appointed new rooms was built specifically for grace-and-favour use, in contrast to other apartments that had been carved out of the older areas of the palace.

Lessels also continued the process of beautification of the interior, notably in the Horn Room, where the stairs were renewed, and in the extensive repairs to the ceiling of the Great Watching Chamber next door. The so-called Wolsey Closet, with its enigmatic overlapping series of panel paintings, was restored by Lessels after it came into the public domain in 1886, when it ceased to be part of a grace-and-favour apartment. His work, whether designing a boiler-house built in a Tudor style or the refashioning of a coat of arms, was based on an archaeological sensitivity and architectural accuracy that had eluded many of his predecessors but set a new standard for his successors.

## Gardens

By the end of the nineteenth century Hampton Court Palace was not only an object lesson in interior restoration but was leading the fashion for colourful garden displays, notably carpet bedding. The East Front in particular was a riot of colour and crowded with bedding plants. Although the fashion waned and a greater variety of planting was introduced, the gardens remained a showcase for the style. The palace gardeners were praised in the *Journal of Horticulture* in 1910 for being "courageous enough in these days of the craze for 'wild gardening' and all the varieties of free informal gardening, to provide those of us who are catholic enough to love all styles of gardening, so long as it is good, with a fine 'carpet bed'". Against this close-set planting was the vast, and influential, herbaceous border along the whole of the East Front garden (fig. 145). Measuring 3 m (10 ft) in width, and over 365 m (400 yds) in length, it was the pride of the palace gardeners. Wilder and with more herbaceous plants and shrubs in the southern section, more formal and planted with bulbs in the northern section, the border was – and remains – a draw for garden visitors.

The Hampton Court garden styles were much copied and very much admired; during the First World War, when the flower gardens were neglected, there was a general outcry. Once the wartime austerity was over, there were moves not only to restore the gardens to their colourful pre-war state but also to revive even earlier forms – or at least, design and plant 1920s interpretations of them.

THE KNOT GARDEN

COTTON LAVENDER
THYME
WINTER SAVORY
LAVENDER
BOX
FLOWERS
PATHS

The Elizabethan Knot Garden, laid out in 1924 (fig. 154), and the Pond Garden, both on the south side of the palace, were Ernest Law's proudest individual contributions to the gardening scene. The Pond Garden was left looking, he believed, "very much as it did when Henry VIII strolled therein with Anne Boleyn". It was "a spot of the daintiest and rarest beauty, the product of nigh four centuries of care and time". Although Law devoted considerable time and energy to understanding the history of the palace and gardens, his romantic sensibilities often led him away from documentary reality. His 1891 description of the Privy Garden is wrong on most counts, as much of what he described was either nineteenth-century or the result of allowing trees to grow unrestrained. Yet his planting schemes were an honest attempt to evoke the spirit of the place:

These gardens retain, indeed, more perhaps of the form and spirit of former days than any others in England, the grounds being laid out in a way suited to the variability of our climate: for winter, walled parterres and sheltered alleys, or summer, grassy banks and plots, shady bowers and nooks, refreshing fountains and flowery arbours – all of which give it an air of repose and seclusion, and an irresistible charm, entirely unattainable by the most lavish expenditure and display of modern horticultural art.

As so often at Hampton Court Palace, the heart ruled the head. The romance and beauty of the place attracted both those who worked on the buildings and estate and those who visited. Archaeological accuracy and romance were interlinked. The twentieth century saw the process continuing, but with a shift in emphasis towards more 'correct' forms of presentation and display.

# *Conservation* in the **TWENTIETH** Century *and beyond*

The process of rediscovery of the past and improved presentation of the palace continues to excite scholars and draw visitors. The palace ceases to be a grace-and-favour residence and, with the establishment of Historic Royal Palaces, is placed under special care.

*156. Excavation of the moat bridge under way in 1910. A trial hole in 1908 had confirmed the existence of features just below the surface.*

*157. The restoration of battlements, pinnacles and beasts on the moat bridge and the retaining wall of the moat, following the excavation of 1910. It was first proposed to put plain foliated finials on the pinnacles as it was not known how they originally terminated. However, at the eleventh hour, Ernest Law "discovered" the original accounts for the making of the Tudor 'beestes' at the Public Record Office and took full credit for this in an article published in The Times in March 1911. The following month a letter from W.H. St John Hope in Country Life alleged that Law had gone "too far" in his claims and that a paper on the bridge at Hampton Court had been read before the Society of Antiquaries the previous year in which the accounts in question had been quoted in full.*

## New directions

Each generation has recast Hampton Court in its own image. In her 1950 book on the palace gardens, Mollie Sands thought that even with modern amenities the grounds had not "broken with the past". As "you walk through them you are reminded at every turn of their former owners". Those "former owners" were just as often custodians or superintendents as monarchs. In the course of the twentieth century, tastes and sensibilities changed, reflected at each stage in the development of the buildings and the gardens. The emphasis now has moved gradually away from restoration of what was once there (or perhaps what it was felt *should* have been there) towards being informed and conserving as much as possible of what has survived.

### *Ernest Law*

The presiding genius over the palace for a generation was Ernest Law, self-appointed guardian of Hampton Court and its history from the close of the nineteenth century until his death in 1930. A former solicitor and himself a grace-and-favour resident in the Pavilion in Home Park, he invested every ounce of his energy in the palace he loved. His touch was everywhere. He planned and implemented new forms of presentation and visitor amenities. He supervised archaeology and the reconstruction of parts of the building and the gardens. He wrote palace guidebooks (an activity in which he enjoyed a monopoly). In 1885–89 he had published his magisterial three-volume history of Hampton Court, which remained until 2003 the most significant study of the palace.

During the Second World War the Grinling Gibbons carvings in the State Apartments were dismantled and put in concrete bunkers in the Lower Orangery.

A comprehensive programme of repairs and rebuilding was carried out on the decorative brick chimneys in the 1970s and 1980s. The total number of chimneys is 241.

In 1984 Prince Charles made his famous speech at Hampton Court criticizing modern architecture for its ugliness and insensitivity.

One of the most apparent of Law's legacies is the moat and the reclaimed bridge that provides the principal entrance to the palace at the Great Gatehouse. The moat had been filled in as part of the works undertaken for William and Mary, in order to make a grand circular turning sweep for carriages. Excavations in 1872 showed that at least part of the bridge survived, and in 1909–10 the decision was taken to investigate and if possible reinstate both moat and bridge (fig. 156). Edward VII (1901–1910) took a personal interest in the plan, while Law wrested control from his colleagues, determined to achieve a complete restoration. Most of the bridge had in fact survived except its parapets, and these were restored complete with ten newly carved Tudor heraldic beasts to the plan described in the original

ABOVE LEFT 158. *The Tudor Kitchens in the 1920s. Visitors then had little sense of the scale or uniqueness of their survival. Only when Lady Baden-Powell's grace-and-favour apartment in the western half of the kitchen was dismantled after she relinquished it in 1974 could the full extent of the ancient kitchen be appreciated.*

LEFT 159. *The tapestry restoration workshop was located in the Queen's Guard Chamber in the 1930s. Hampton Court Palace has been one of the world's leading centres for tapestry repair and conservation throughout the twentieth century.*

ABOVE 160. *The palace's Clerk of Works with one of the bosses removed from the Great Hall roof during repairs in the 1920s. A carvers' workshop was set up in the Upper Orangery in the King's Apartments where the bosses, carved heads and other decorative elements from the roof were stored and repaired while the structural work was being carried out in the hall.*

building accounts (fig. 157). (These carvings weathered badly, and the present beasts date from 1950.) The parapets include discarded Tudor bricks found in the moat, while the gatehouse itself was refaced again, in a more mellow brick than before. The century was opening at Hampton Court as it would continue, with a new emphasis on archaeology and the reuse of historic material.

Law was also instrumental in opening up more areas inside the palace for visitors (fig. 158). In 1917–18 he created what is now the 'Tudor route', passing out of the Great Hall via the Horn Room through the Great Watching Chamber and along the Haunted Gallery to the Royal Pew. Works in the Horn Room involved opening long-blocked doorways and rehanging the antlers and horns that were discovered in a heap at the foot of the serving stairs. Although resigned to the permanent public use of the Haunted Gallery, the grace-and-favour residents objected bitterly to the proposed opening of the upper part of the Chapel Royal. Lady Rossmore shuddered at the prospect of the "hundreds of dirty, smelly unwashed that will tramp through during the week", so fouling the space that "we, none of us, could even try to sit any service out". Despite these protestations, public access came first.

The Great Hall was the object of the most thorough programme of works, after dry rot and beetle infestation were found in the roof in 1922. Decayed timbers were replaced and a steel truss system was inserted into the hammerbeam roof structure (fig. 160). The painted decoration on the timber was stripped away, as were many of the corbels, armour and other

the pictures on the walls the principal or even the sole objects of public and professional admiration. The palace's keepers and their advisers increasingly aimed to provide a more appropriate historic context for surviving grand and rare items of furniture, such as the state beds.

Queen Mary, the wife of George V, had a deep personal interest in Kensington Palace; she also took a hand in the presentation of Hampton Court through gifts and advice following public criticism of the state of the furnishings in 1921 (fig. 163). Considerable improvements were made in the course of the 1930s, culminating in a thorough re-presentation of the State Apartments on more historically appropriate lines. Sir Philip Sassoon gave suitable furnishings, among them chairs of state to be placed in their proper setting beneath the throne canopies. He persuaded other philanthropists to provide improved amenities such as heating, ordered new wall hangings and rationalized the hitherto indiscriminate use of protective barriers. Kenneth Clark, Surveyor of the King's Pictures, undertook a thorough rehanging programme of the paintings. Elements of the basically chronological sequence that he devised still remain. In 1938, on the eve of war, Queen Mary attended a garden party to mark the centenary of the palace's opening to the public and the completion of this major re-presentation scheme.

### The glory of the gardens

The gardens remained the most popular attraction of the palace. The glorious, labour-intensive borders and beds with their seasonal displays drew crowds of admirers. The largest new addition to the public areas came with the opening of the Tiltyard Gardens in 1925. Originally the site of the Tudor jousting arena, from which a single brick viewing tower has survived, the 3.2 hectares (8 acres) had been made into a royal kitchen and fruit garden in the reigns of William III and Anne. In the late nineteenth century, after the palace gardens had ceased to provide food for the royal table, the Tiltyard was leased to a successful nursery, which provided the vast numbers of plants required annually for the famous bedding displays.

Eventually the lease was terminated, in order to make the Tiltyard into a new visitor amenity with tennis courts, tea-rooms and new garden displays. The tea-rooms and cafeteria were the most successful element in the scheme, and their successor (built in 1964 and refurbished in 1995) still welcomes

*164. The palace electricity master board in 1954. Gradually every modern convenience has been added to the ancient building, from sewers, gas and electricity to computer cabling.*

novelties that Jesse had introduced in 1844. Almost as soon as the work on the Great Hall was completed, the roof of the Chapel Royal was found to be in a similarly decayed and dangerous state. Here, too, new structural supports were introduced to bear the weight of the Tudor timber ceiling.

### Opening new areas

Gradually, from the 1920s, other parts of the palace were opened to public view: the Wolsey Rooms in 1951 after an attempted opening in 1923 was halted following complaints that visitors' footsteps disturbed the composure of the resident below, the Orangery in 1931, the Tennis Court in 1949, the Cumberland Suite in 1963 (fig. 162) and the Banqueting House in 1983. Styles of presentation of the historic spaces were also changing. No longer were

165. *A palace admission ticket. The one-shilling (5 p) entry charge was introduced in 1912 and survived until the post-1970 inflationary spiral. The palace has been open seven days a week since 1930.*

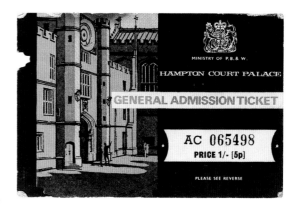

visitors. The present car park opened in the 1930s on the former parade ground behind the Barrack Block, just below the Tiltyard Gardens. This removed the unsightly serried ranks of cars and charabancs previously parked at the West Front of the palace (fig. 146).

In the wider estate, Home Park had been opened to the public in 1893, when it finally ceased to be a royal stud. It soon acquired both a public golf course and a model yacht pond, each with a clubhouse. Bushy Park, a focus of Chestnut Sunday gatherings and penny-farthing bicycle races, had been open for well over half a century. Both parks were extensively used for growing crops in each of the world wars, as were the palace gardens.

## Wartime

In the Second World War, anti-glider trenches were dug in Home Park to deter enemy landings, and the palace was the target of a number of (largely unsuccessful) bombing raids. The worst occasion was when up to 300 incendiary bombs fell on the East Front on the night of 26 September 1940, although most were swiftly extinguished and damage was minimal. As a precaution, many important paintings were subsequently evacuated to safe locations, in particular the National Library of Wales at Aberystwyth, or were placed in secure stores. A photographic record was made of important decorative elements such as the Grinling Gibbons carvings, and copies of the murals in the Baroque apartments were made.

The US Eighth Army subsequently took over part of Bushy Park as its headquarters in 1942 and General Eisenhower later planned the 1944 D-Day landings there. The soldiers enjoyed being entertained in the palace – although some repaid the compliment by leaving their mark in the form of graffiti in sensitive areas such as the soft stonework in Fountain Court.

### From living palace to ancient monument

Once the Second World War was over, the palace and grounds swiftly returned to their former role as escape valve for many Londoners. Paintings came back from storage and more of the palace was opened up. Although facilities for visitors improved gradually over the post-war years, especially as leisure time expanded, there was demand for more. Change was in the air.

Ideas about historic houses were shifting, not least as England's stately homes were opening their doors and garden gates in order to make ends meet. In the visitor market for historic houses there was major competition. Meanwhile, the palace community itself was altering and shrinking. New tenants were not so easily found for grace-and-favour residences, while the total number of apartments was reduced both to save money and to be able to provide improved amenities for the remainder. Fewer of the residents kept servants. One symbol of change was that the infants' school in Tennis Court Lane closed its doors in 1953 (fig. 166).

Two highly significant and related decisions were made in 1969. First, the increasingly outmoded tradition of grace-and-favour residence would be allowed to draw to its natural close. With the rise of the welfare state and the demise of Empire it was seen as an anachronism, and no further apartments would be allocated or created.

Secondly, Hampton Court would become an Ancient Monument and would no longer be considered a 'living' palace. Responsibility for its upkeep was to be transferred from the Royal Household to the Department of Ancient Monuments and Historic Buildings. In future, funding would be put towards the preservation of the 'unoccupied' palace within its setting and better presentation to the visiting public (fig. 167). The scene was set for the major shift on both counts that has been the hallmark of the palace since the 1970s.

### Shifting emphasis

In-depth research, conservation measures for both the buildings and their contents, and a coherent

166. *Proposal for the new infants' school and mistresses' residence in Tennis Court Lane, 1876, which served the resident palace community until 1953.*

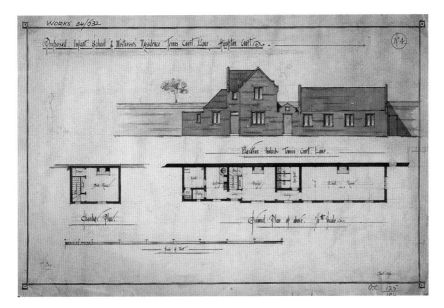

ABOVE 167. *Restoration of the Verrio murals on the King's Staircase in 1968. The first restoration programmes took place in the mid-eighteenth century, only twenty years after the paintings had been completed, and these delicate works have received attention at regular intervals since.*

RIGHT 168. *Restoration of the Tijou screen by Mr English in March 1950. A blacksmith's workshop was built around the individual screens where all but the most sensitive work took place. The ironwork is exceptionally delicate, and there have been many repair schemes over its lifetime. The current scheme of repair is partly complete.*

approach to displaying the palace and gardens to the public all played their part in post-1969 Hampton Court. Under the plan devised by Harold Yexley, the senior architect in the Department of Ancient Monuments and Historic Buildings, some £2 million was allocated to be spent between 1974 and 1980 on improving facilities, enhancing the historic spaces and completing the visitor routes.

Various ways were found of using the increasing amounts of vacant space, whether by opening them to public view, taking in tenants with useful craft skills or as offices for palace staff. A more considered and historically inspired approach was taken to the display of the interiors, and especially the pictures. These included the enhanced presentation in 1975 of the prized and newly conserved Mantegna series of the *Triumphs of Caesar* in the Lower Orangery, and new galleries for the reserve collection of paintings in rooms on the palace's south-east corner, which opened in 1980. Finally, in 1984 a dedicated Renaissance Picture Gallery opened on the south side of Base Court, beyond the Wolsey Rooms,

with environmental controls for the display of early works from the Royal Collection.

In tandem with all this, a more rigorously conservation-minded approach to the palace itself was adopted from the 1970s. One of the most visible results of the shift was – as usual for this building – in the brickwork. Brick repairs using mass-produced reproduction Tudor bricks had given many areas a wholly unfortunate new appearance. The repairs were in future to be carried out with handmade, traditional Bulmer bricks, bonded with lime mortar rather than Portland cement. A rolling programme of recording and making good the Tudor brickwork – often replacing inappropriate later work – continues to this day.

## Fire and its aftermath

A watershed came in 1986. At dawn on Easter Day, 31 March, fire swept through the third floor and the roof on the South Front (fig. 171). It had begun in the apartment of Lady Gale, located above the King's State Apartments, and the lack of fire compartments in the roof void coupled with a failure of the alarm system allowed the blaze to race through the length of the building. Regrettably, Lady Gale perished in the fire, which may have been started by an unguarded candle flame in her bedroom.

The danger of fire had always been recognized – as early as 1716 wooden chimneypieces were replaced by stone – and there had been major incidents before, notably in 1882, 1886 and again in 1952 in the Cumberland Suite (fig. 169). The palace had even had its own fire brigade, instituted in 1876 (and disbanded in 1954/5) (fig. 170). None of these disasters matched the 1986 fire in the seriousness of the damage.

While firemen on twenty fire tenders were tackling the flames, a much-practised salvage operation swung into action and a dedicated team was able to remove almost all of the valuable and portable works of art. Only one table and one painting were consumed by the fire. News pictures of the scenes of devastation flashed round the world, showing leaping flames and, later, roof timbers and Grinling Gibbons limewood carvings in charred piles (fig. 172). By early afternoon, the fire had been extinguished and The Queen was touring the site to see the damage for herself.

The fire and its aftermath ushered in a further era of re-presentation and restoration at the palace, as well as a heightened awareness of the fragility and importance of its historic fabric. An archaeological approach was applied to the wreckage: for example, all fragments were meticulously examined and recorded, and many were rescued, repaired and reused despite the damage they had sustained. This approach proved to be a model for other historic properties, since the

ABOVE LEFT 169. *Firemen on the roof above the Cumberland Suite in 1952. One newspaper reported the following day, "Thirty titled women who live in the grace and favour apartments of the palace heard the crackling of burning wood just before 8 o'clock." The firemen were able to tackle the blaze using the builders' scaffolding that had previously been erected in Clock Court.*

ABOVE 170. *The palace fire brigade on the West Front, 1954. Ernest Law, writing at the end of the nineteenth century, recorded, "The Fire Brigade now consists of a Superintendent and eighteen men, six of whom are resident within the Palace, and all of whom live close by. They have weekly practices; are regularly drilled once a month; and periodically inspected by an experienced officer, specially selected for this service."*

ABOVE RIGHT 171. *Aerial view of the South Front showing the fire damage, 31 March 1986. Much of the roof, 60 m (200 ft) long, had collapsed, sending timbers and molten lead crashing through the ceilings into the King's State Apartments below. The building was extensively fire-damaged, filled with tons of waterlogged debris, open to the elements and inherently unstable without its roof.*

RIGHT 172. *Firemen in the smouldering ruins of the Cartoon Gallery, 1 April 1986. Fortuitously, the Acts of the Apostles tapestries that had been hanging in the gallery had been removed for cleaning prior to the fire. Reconstruction of the damaged interiors had to wait nearly three years to allow the building to dry out after the deluge from the firemen's hoses.*

TOP 173. *The West Closet, the King's Private Apartments, photographed in 1982 in its last incarnation before the fully researched scheme of the early 1990s.*

ABOVE 174. *The West Closet, the King's Private Apartments, photographed in 1999. The re-presentation following the 1986 fire returned the King's Apartments to as close a state as could be determined from archival and archaeological evidence to their appearance in about 1700.*

response to subsequent serious fires at Uppark, West Sussex (1989), and at Windsor Castle (1992) was able to draw on the experience at Hampton Court. Detailed historical investigation, both through archival research and archaeology, would henceforth precede and inform both repair and reconstruction.

### Re-presentation schemes

The most visible and splendid fruit of that approach in the first half of the 1990s was the restoration and display of the King's Apartments themselves (figs. 173, 174). This was accompanied by work on the Tudor Kitchens, the Cumberland Suite and the Queen's Private Apartments, as well as the identification of the 'Tudor route' in the rooms beyond the Great Hall. The *Triumphs of Caesar* paintings were redisplayed too, in a re-creation of the gallery at San Sebastiano where they originally hung. Finally came the restoration to its original form of the Privy Garden beneath the King's State Apartments.

These have been among the most influential changes in a major historic house in the modern age. In re-presenting the King's Apartments, there was opportunity to re-create the original form and decoration of the *enfilade* of rooms: the visitor now moves from the fairly public Guard Chamber to the very private bedchamber and study above, and then through the suites of more intimate rooms below. Furniture, paintings and tapestries were returned to the rooms for which they were originally intended. Historians in the 1980s were promoting the importance of spaces and their uses in the rituals of royal households as an expression of the politics that underpinned them. Here at Hampton Court was a unique opportunity to regain the ritual significance of the rooms, their disposition and decoration.

One of the most visible changes in the State Apartments was the rehanging of tapestries that had been dispersed long before, either elsewhere within the palace or to other royal houses, and replaced with wallpapers. The programme of cleaning and repair of these precious objects was the finest hour of the palace's Textile Conservation Studio, a body that could trace its origins back to William Morris's tapestry company three quarters of a century earlier (figs. 159, 177). The fortuitous discovery and subsequent permanent loan of late seventeenth-century copies of the famed Raphael cartoons, which would hang in the restored Cartoon Gallery, released the *Acts of the Apostles* tapestries for display in the King's and Queen's Apartments.

These rooms were ceremonially reopened in July 1992. Just as influential were the Tudor Kitchens, opened to the public the previous year. In the 1970s they had been cleared of later insertions that provided grace-and-favour accommodation. Revealed was a kitchen block on a dramatic scale that has its

175. *The restoration of the Privy Garden was a major, and an innovative, exercise in garden archaeology. This view shows progress at October 1993. The upper garden was excavated in the summer of 1993 and the lower garden the following spring. The results exceeded all expectations. Discoveries included brick bases for the statue plinths as well as the foundations of the central steps, tree pit positions on the terraces and the entire original drainage system, which was repaired and put back into service.*

176. *The restored Privy Garden today. The palace under William and Mary had been conceived as the centrepiece of a great Baroque landscape. The original vistas were now restored and for the first time in two centuries it was possible both to view the South Front as Wren intended and to see the river from the King's Apartments as William III had demanded.*

origins in the earliest Tudor house on the site, built by Lord Daubeney. The displays have ranks of replica food, a vast roaring log fire and even a re-creation of a slaughterhouse. In more recent years a band of costumed kitchen presenters and 'living archaeologists' has been contributing to both visitor enjoyment and knowledge about historic kitchen practices.

### The Privy Garden

Once the work had been completed on the King's Apartments, attention turned to the Privy Garden

outside. Allowed, then encouraged, over the years to become filled with overgrown trees and secluded walkways, this garden was also to be returned to its original glory. The scheme reunited the design of buildings and gardens for the first time in 250 years. The Victorian shrubs were felled, and important specimens were taken away for propagation or reuse.

Archaeological excavations revealed that just below the surface still lay the bones of William III's great Baroque garden (fig. 175). Even the shapes

of beds and borders could be discerned, while pictorial and documentary evidence provided the necessary detail. Beginning in 1992, and completed three years later, the transformation was total and spectacular (fig. 176). Historic plant varieties were grown in Britain and The Netherlands. Some 33,000 box plants formed the edging to the beds cut into nearly a hectare (2 acres) of turf. Queen Mary's Bower was rebuilt in green oak on its high terrace to the west and replanted with hornbeam, replacements were carved for the original statuary (brought indoors for preservation), and a programme of restoration was begun on Tijou's screen on the river edge. Channel 4 News acquired the rights to document the restoration project, and its regular broadcasts on progress helped engage public interest still further. In ten years the gardens have matured into a scene that William III and Anne would have readily recognized.

*Gardens and garden features*

The fame of the Hampton Court Palace gardens has continued to spread, while a more comprehensive strategy for care and renewal has been adopted since the late 1990s. The gardens are the home of the National Collection of heliotropes, a quintessentially Victorian flower that attests to Hampton Court's nineteenth-century renown. As the avenues of trees in the parkland have reached the end of their natural lives, so they too have been replaced in successive programmes of work. The Cross Avenue and the Long Water Avenue in Home Park have both been replanted with lime trees of the appropriate species, descendants of the originals brought from The Netherlands in the later seventeenth century. The importance of the Baroque gardens is reflected in the plans to reinstate Queen Mary II's prized collection of exotic plants, as well as a continuing programme to make replicas of the Delftware vases that she commissioned to display plants and flowers indoors.

The most recent addition to the garden ensemble was installed in 2002: the Jubilee Fountain at the end of the Long Water (fig. 178). Its five jets symbolize the five decades of The Queen's reign. Over the years the fountains in the gardens have been more troublesome than spectacular, suffering from lack of water pressure. Today that problem has been overcome in fine fashion.

TOP 177. *The Textile Conservation Studio's 'washing machine' housed in a greenhouse 24 m (80 ft) in length to the north of the palace. The late-nineteenth-century policy of restoration of tapestries, even reweaving whole sections, has been superseded in recent decades by a policy of painstaking cleaning and repair.*

ABOVE 178. *The Jubilee Fountain at the far end of the Long Water, created to mark the Golden Jubilee of HM Queen Elizabeth II in 2002. This is the largest multi-jet fountain in Britain.*

RIGHT 179. *Cleaning the pendants on the ceiling of the Chapel Royal and bringing back life to one of the most fantastical legacies of the age of Henry VIII. Historic Royal Palaces has a team of conservators who use both traditional techniques and cutting-edge science in their guardianship of the interiors and the objects they contain.*

## Historic Royal Palaces

The new style of thinking and display since the 1980s was accompanied by organizational change. In 1989 the palace and the other 'unoccupied' royal palaces – the Tower of London, Kensington Palace State Apartments, Kew Palace with Queen Charlotte's Cottage, and the Banqueting House in

ABOVE 180. *The Hampton Court Flower Show is an annual crowd-pulling summer event.*

RIGHT 181. *HM Queen Elizabeth II is greeted by costumed interpreters taking the parts of the disputatious clerics of 1604 at the commemoration of the 400th anniversary of the Hampton Court Conference, 12 May 2004. Historic Royal Palaces was one of the first heritage bodies in Britain to introduce live interpreters, and Hampton Court remains one of the most important venues for authentic costumed presentation both in the formal historic spaces and in the kitchens.*

## A touchstone of English history

What is Hampton Court Palace today? It is a major visitor attraction, for people from both Britain and overseas. The modern high point in numbers of paying visitors came with the major re-presentations of the early 1990s, when more than half a million people a year passed through the palace doors. This figure now stands at some 400,000 a year, reduced partly by the uncertain international situation since 2001. An even greater number visits the gardens and the parks; as an entrance charge is now made for the main areas of the historic garden – and the Maze continues high in popularity – the considerable costs of their maintenance are being recouped.

The palace is the principal office location for Historic Royal Palaces. Many former grace-and-favour residences that are not appropriate for display to the public now house staff offices. Various long-standing tenants, notably the Royal School of Needlework and the Embroiderers' Guild, occupy other apartments. In the summer months Base Court is the venue for the Hampton Court Music Festival, and Home Park accommodates the Royal Horticultural Society's Hampton Court Palace Flower Show (fig. 180). Both events continue the tradition of popular entertainment alongside the historic attraction that has underpinned the visitor's experience since the nineteenth century.

Hampton Court Palace is more than a visitor attraction, a historic house or an out-of-the-ordinary office building. It is one of the touchstones of English history. With the possible exception of Windsor Castle, nowhere else may visitors see the full complex of a surviving ancient royal palace. Certainly no other place may claim such an intimate relationship with Henry VIII, one of the most powerful and recognizable of English monarchs. Nowhere else in England does the full range of a Baroque royal palace survive. If William III and Mary II are less well known than their Tudor predecessors, their influence is internationally famous through the buildings and gardens at Hampton Court.

Hampton Court Palace embodies some of the great stories and greatest figures of English history. The palace was built on a gigantic scale, designed both to reflect the status and glory of its owners and to accommodate a huge number of people when the royal court was in residence. Art and architecture combined to make a grand statement of power. Once that need disappeared after the court ceased to reside there, the palace entered a new life as both a collection of residences and a draw for visitors. A history of tourism is visible at Hampton Court. A mission for educators, archaeologists and conservationists is also visible there: to understand the buildings, their contents and their history, and to pass them on to future generations.

Whitehall – were brought together under one body. No longer to be managed by the Department of the Environment (successor to the Ministry of Public Buildings and Works), they were now to be run by a separate agency. The Historic Royal Palaces Agency was less constrained by the demands of Whitehall and the annual budget round.

Hampton Court Palace was able to strike out more boldly and in new directions, among them the use of costumed guides to interpret the historic spaces for visitors (the first time the experiment had been tried at a major British site) (fig. 181). Simon Thurley, the architectural historian who was appointed the Agency's first Curator in 1990, led many of these projects and was a tireless advocate for the palace during his six-year tenure.

This distancing from direct government oversight has continued to increase. Nine years later, the agency status ended and Historic Royal Palaces became an independent charity. It has a royal charter to pursue the twin goals of conservation and education – both broadly defined – in maintaining and presenting the five major historic properties in its care (fig. 179). Historic Royal Palaces continues to fulfil its charitable purposes in caring for these great buildings, doing so without financial support from the public purse or the royal purse through income from admissions and retail profits.

# FURTHER READING

T. Campbell, 'Cardinal Wolsey's tapestry collection', *Antiquaries Journal* 76, 1996, pp. 73–137

H. Colvin (ed), *The History of the King's Works*, vol. IV (1982) and vol. V (1976), London (HMSO)

B. Dolman, *Drama and Debate at the Court of James I*, London (Historic Royal Palaces) 2004

D. Ford and M. Turner, 'The Kynges New Haull: A response to Jonathan Foyle's "A Reconstruction of Thomas Wolsey's Great Hall at Hampton Court Palace"', *Architectural History*, vol. 47, 2004, pp. 53–76

J. Foyle, 'A Reconstruction of Thomas Wolsey's Great Hall at Hampton Court Palace', *Architectural History*, vol. 45, 2002, pp. 128–58

E. Law, *A History of Hampton Court Palace*, 3 vols., London (George Bell & Sons) 1903

P. Lindsay, *Hampton Court: A History*, London (Meridian) 1948

T. Longstaffe-Gowan, *The Gardens and Parks at Hampton Court Palace*, London (Frances Lincoln) 2005

S. Parker, *Grace and Favour: The Hampton Court Palace Community, 1750–1950*, London (Historic Royal Palaces) 2005

S. Thurley (ed), *The King's Privy Garden at Hampton Court Palace, 1689–1995*, London (Apollo/Historic Royal Palaces) 1995

S. Thurley, *Hampton Court: A Social and Architectural History*, New Haven CT and London (Yale University Press) 2003

# INDEX

# ACKNOWLEDGEMENTS

# PICTURE CREDITS

The authors and publishers would like to thank all those members of the staff of Historic Royal Palaces (HRP) and others who have contributed in any way to the preparation of this book. Particular thanks are due to Anthony Geraghty, Tara Hambling, Gordon Higgott, Edward Impey, Todd Longstaffe-Gowan and Simon Thurley, and to the curators' team at HRP, especially Brett Dolman, Sebastian Edwards, Susanne Groom, Susan Holmes and Kent Rawlinson. Many thanks are also due to Annie Heron for obtaining illustrations, to Jonathan Foyle for drawing the plans (inside front cover) and to Back2Front Photography, Robin Forster (assisted by Tim Whittaker and Ian Forster), Nick Guttridge and Andreas von Einsiedel for photography. The authors' special thanks go to HRP's Publications Manager, Clare Murphy, for initiating the project, managing the picture research and editing the text.

First published in 2005 by Merrell Publishers Limited

Head office:
81 Southwark Street
London SE1 0HX

New York office:
49 West 24th Street, 8th floor
New York, 10010

www.merrellpublishers.com

in association with

Historic Royal Palaces
Hampton Court Palace
Surrey KT8 9AU

www.hrp.org.uk

Text copyright © 2005 Historic Royal Palaces
Pictures copyright © 2005 the copyright holders (see right)

British Library Cataloguing-in-Publication data:
Worsley, Lucy
    Hampton Court Palace : the official illustrated history
    1.Hampton Court Palace (Richmond upon Thames, London, England) –
    I.Title II.Souden, David
    942.1'95

ISBN 1 85894 282 9

Edited by Clare Murphy and Elisabeth Ingles
Indexed by Hilary Bird
Designed by Maggi Smith

Printed and bound in China